Pat Barker

NEW BRITISH FICTION

Series editors:
Philip Tew
Rod Mengham

Published
Sonya Andermahr: **Jeanette Winterson**
Bradley Buchanan: **Hanif Kureishi**
Frederick M. Holmes: **Julian Barnes**
Kaye Mitchell: **A. L. Kennedy**
Robert Morace: **Irvine Welsh**
Stephen Morton: **Salman Rushdie**
Mark Rawlinson: **Pat Barker**
Philip Tew: **Zadie Smith**
Lynn Wells: **Ian McEwan**

Forthcoming
Gerard Barrett: **Graham Swift**
Sebastian Groes: **Martin Amis**
Rod Mengham: **Jonathan Coe**
Mark Wormald: **Kazuo Ishiguro**

New British Fiction Series
Series Standing Order

ISBN 1–4039–4274–9 hardback
ISBN 1–4039–4275–7 paperback
(*outside North America only*)

You can receive future titles in this series as they are published by placing a standing order. Please contact your bookseller or, in case of difficulty, write to us at the address below with your name and address, the title of the series and the ISBN quoted above.

Customer Services Department, Palgrave Ltd
Houndmills, Basingstoke, Hampshire RG21 6XS, England

NEW BRITISH FICTION

Pat Barker

Mark Rawlinson

palgrave
macmillan

First published 2010 by
PALGRAVE MACMILLAN

Palgrave Macmillan in the UK is an imprint of Macmillan Publishers Limited, registered in England, company number 785998, of Houndmills, Basingstoke, Hampshire RG21 6XS.

Palgrave Macmillan in the US is a division of St Martin's Press LLC, 175 Fifth Avenue, New York, NY 10010.

Palgrave Macmillan is the global academic imprint of the above companies and has companies and representatives throughout the world.

Palgrave® and Macmillan® are registered trademarks in the United States, the United Kingdom, Europe and other countries.

ISBN-13: 978–0–230–00179–4 hardback
ISBN-13: 978–0–230–00180–0 paperback

This book is printed on paper suitable for recycling and made from fully managed and sustained forest sources. Logging, pulping and manufacturing processes are expected to conform to the environmental regulations of the country of origin.

A catalogue record for this book is available from the British Library.

A catalog record for this book is available from the Library of Congress.

10   9   8   7   6   5   4   3   2   1
19 18 17 16 15 14 13 12 11 10

Printed and bound in China

CONTENTS

GENERAL EDITORS' PREFACE

This series highlights with its very title two crucial elements in the nature of contemporary British fiction, especially as a field for academic research and study. The first term indicates the originality and freshness of such writing expressed in a huge formal diversity. The second evokes the cultural identity of the authors included, who nevertheless represent through their diversity a challenge to any hegemonic or narrow view of Britishness. As regards the fiction, many of the writers featured in this series continue to draw from and adapt long traditions of cultural and aesthetic practice. Such aesthetic continuities contrast starkly with the conditions of knowledge at the end of the twentieth century and the beginning of the twenty-first, a period that has been characterized by an apprehension of radical presentness, a sense of unprecedented forms of experience and an obsession with new modes of self-awareness. This stage of the survival of the novel may perhaps be best remembered as a millennial and post-millennial moment, a time of fluctuating reading practices and of historical events whose impact is largely still unresolved. The new fiction of these times reflects a rapidly changing cultural and ideological reality, as well as a renewal of the commitment of both writers and readers to both the relevance and utility of narrative forms of knowledge.

Each volume in this series will serve as an introductory guide to an individual author chosen from a list of those whose work has proved to be of general interest to reviewers, academics, students and the general reading public. Each volume will offer information concerning the life, work and literary and cultural contexts appropriate to the chosen subject of each book; individual volumes will share the same overall structure with a largely common organization of materials. The result is intended to be suitable for both academic and general readers: putting accessibility at a premium, without compromising an ambitious series of readings of today's

viiGENERAL EDITORS' PREFACE

most vitally interesting British novelists, interpreting their work, assessing their influences, and exploring their relationship to the times in which they live.

Philip Tew and Rod Mengham

ACKNOWLEDGEMENTS

The author would like to thank Pat Barker for her kind assistance in the completion of this book.

PART I

Introduction

TIMELINE

1960   Harold Macmillan 'Winds of Change' speech, Cape
Town, South Africa
John F. Kennedy elected as US President
Aged six, Kazuo Ishiguro arrives in Britain

1961   Adolf Eichmann on trial in Israel for role in Holocaust
Bay of Pigs: attempted invasion of Cuba
Berlin Wall constructed
Yuri Gagarin first person in Space
Silicon chip patented
Private Eye magazine begins publication
Muriel Spark, *The Prime of Miss Jean Brodie*
Jonathan Coe born

1962   Cuban Missile Crisis
Marilyn Monroe dies
Independence for Uganda; followed this decade by Kenya
(1963), Northern Rhodesia (1964), Southern Rhodesia
(1965), Barbados (1966)

1963   John F. Kennedy assassinated in Dallas
Martin Luther King Jr delivers 'I Have a Dream' speech
Profumo Affair
Joan Littlewood and Theatre Workshop present *O, What a Lovely War* at the Theatre Royal, Stratford East

1964   Nelson Mandela sentenced to life imprisonment
Commercial pirate radio challenges BBC monopoly

1965   State funeral of Winston Churchill
US sends troops to Vietnam
A. L. Kennedy born in Dundee, Scotland

1966   Ian Brady and Myra Hindley sentenced to life imprisonment for Moors Murders
England beats West Germany 4–2 at Wembley to win Football World Cup
Star Trek series debut on NBC television
Jean Rhys, *The Wide Sargasso Sea*

1967   Six-Day War in the Middle East
World's first heart transplant
Abortion Act legalizes termination of pregnancy in UK
Sergeant Pepper's Lonely Hearts Club Band album released by The Beatles
Flann O'Brien, *The Third Policeman*

1968   Anti-Vietnam War protestors attempt to storm American Embassy in Grosvenor Square
Martin Luther King Jr assassinated
Robert F. Kennedy assassinated
Student protests and riots in France
Lord Chamberlain's role as censor of plays in the UK is abolished
Lindsay Anderson, *If . . .*

1969   Civil rights march in Northern Ireland attacked by Protestants
Apollo 11 lands on the Moon with Neil Armstrong's famous first steps

Rock concert at Woodstock
Yasser Arafat becomes leader of PLO
Booker Prize first awarded; winner P. H. Newby,
Something to Answer for
Open University founded in the UK
John Fowles, *The French Lieutenant's Woman*

1970   Popular Front for the Liberation of Palestine (PFLP)
hijacks five planes
Students activists and bystanders shot in anti-Vietnam
War protest at Kent State University, Ohio, four killed,
nine wounded
UK voting age reduced from 21 years to 18

1971   Decimal currency introduced in the UK
Internment without trial of terrorist suspects in
Northern Ireland begins
India and Pakistan in conflict after Bangladesh declares
independence

1972   Miners' strike
Bloody Sunday in Londonderry, 14 protestors killed
outright or fatally wounded by British troops
Aldershot barracks bomb initiates IRA campaign with
seven dead
Britain enters Common Market
Massacre of Israeli athletes at Munich Olympics
Watergate scandal
Controversy over Stanley Kubrick's film of Anthony
Burgess's novel *A Clockwork Orange*
Samuel Beckett, *Not I*

1973   US troops leave Vietnam
Arab–Israeli 15-day Yom Kippur War
PM Edward Heath introduces three-day working week
Martin Amis, *The Rachel Papers*

1974   Miners' strike
IRA bombings in Guildford (five dead) and Birmingham
(21 dead)

1975   Microsoft founded
Sex Discrimination Act
Zadie Smith born in North London
Malcolm Bradbury, *The History Man*
The 'Yorkshire Ripper' killings begin
Paul Fussell's *The Great War and Modern Memory*

1976   Weak economy forces UK government loan from the
International Monetary Fund (IMF)
Ian McEwan, *First Love, Last Rites*

1977   *Star Wars* released
UK unemployment tops 1,600,000
Nintendo begins to sell computer games
Sex Pistols 'Anarchy in the UK' tour

1978   Soviet troops occupy Afghanistan
First test-tube baby born in Oldham, England

1979   Iranian Revolution establishes Islamic theocracy
Margaret Thatcher becomes PM after Conservative
election victory
USSR invades Afghanistan
Lord Mountbatten assassinated by the IRA

1980   Iran–Iraq War starts
Iranian Embassy siege in London
CND rally at Greenham Common airbase, England
IRA hunger strike at Belfast Maze Prison over political
status for prisoners
Julian Barnes, *Metroland*

1981   Prince Charles and Lady Diana marry in St Paul's
Cathedral with 750 million worldwide television
audience
Widespread urban riots in UK including Brixton,
Holloway, Toxteth, Handsworth, Moss Side
AIDS identified
Peter Sutcliffe convicted of the 'Yorkshire Ripper'
murders

First IBM personal computer
Alasdair Gray, *Lanark*
Salman Rushdie, *Midnight's Children*, which wins Booker
Prize for Fiction

1982 Mark Thatcher, PM's son, disappears for three days in
Sahara during the Paris-Dakar rally
Falklands War with Argentina, costing the UK over
£1.6 billion
Body of Roberto Calvi, chairman of Vatican-connected
Banco Ambrosiano, found hanging beneath Blackfriars
Bridge, London
Pat Barker, *Union Street*

1983 Klaus Barbie, Nazi war criminal, arrested in Bolivia
Beirut: US Embassy and barracks bombing, killing
hundreds of members of multinational peacekeeping
force, mostly US marines
US troops invade Grenada
Microsoft Word first released
Salman Rushdie, *Shame*, which wins Prix du Meilleur
Livre Etranger (France)

1984 Miners' strike
HIV identified as cause of AIDS
IRA bomb at Conservative Party Conference in Brighton
kills four
British Telecom privatization shares sale
Thirty-eight deaths during clashes at Liverpool v.
Juventus football match at Heysel Stadium,
Brussels
Martin Amis, *Money: A Suicide Note*
Julian Barnes, *Flaubert's Parrot*
James Kelman, *Busconductor Hines*
Graham Swift, *Waterland*
Pat Barker, *Blow Your House Down*

1985 Famine in Ethiopia and Live Aid concert
Damage to ozone layer discovered

Mikhail Gorbachev becomes Soviet Premier and introduces *glasnost* (openness with the West) and *perestroika* (economic restructuring)
PC Blakelock murdered during riots on Broadwater Farm estate in Tottenham, London
My Beautiful Laundrette film released (dir. Stephen Frears, screenplay Hanif Kureishi)
Jeanette Winterson, *Oranges Are Not the Only Fruit*

1986   Abolition of Greater London Council and other metropolitan county councils in England
Violence between police and protestors at Wapping, East London after Rupert Murdoch sacks 5000 print workers
Challenger shuttle explodes
Chernobyl nuclear accident
US bombs Libya
Peter Ackroyd, *Hawksmoor*
Pat Barker, *The Century's Daughter* (later retitled *Liza's England*)

1987   Capsizing of RORO ferry, *Herald of Free Enterprise*, off Zeebrugge kills 193 people
London Stock Exchange and market collapse on 'Black Monday'
Remembrance Sunday: eleven killed by Provisional IRA bomb in Enniskillen
Ian McEwan, *The Child in Time*, which wins Whitbread Novel Award
Jeanette Winterson, *The Passion*
Chanel Four broadcast Tony Harrison's poem V (1985)
Derek Jarman, dir. *The Last of England*

1988   US shoots down Iranian passenger flight
Pan Am flight 103 bombed over Lockerbie, 270 people killed
Soviet troop withdrawals from Afghanistan begin
Salman Rushdie, *The Satanic Verses*

1989   Fatwa issued against Rushdie by Iranian leadership
(Khomeini)
Fall of Berlin Wall
Exxon Valdez oil disaster
Student protestors massacred in Tiananmen Square,
Beijing
Hillsborough Stadium disaster in which 96 football
fans die
Kazuo Ishiguro, *The Remains of the Day*, which wins
Booker Prize for Fiction
Jeanette Winterson, *Sexing the Cherry*
Pat Barker, *The Man Who Wasn't There*

1990   London poll tax riots
Fall of Thatcher; John Major becomes Conservative PM
Nelson Mandela freed from jail
Jeanette Winterson adapts *Oranges* for BBC television
film
A. S. Byatt, *Possession*
Hanif Kureishi, *The Buddha of Suburbia*, which wins
Whitbread First Novel Prize
A. L. Kennedy, *Night Geometry and the Garscadden Trains*

1991   Soviet Union collapses
First Iraq War with 12-day Operation Desert Storm
Apartheid ended in South Africa
PM Major negotiates opt-out for Britain from European
Monetary Union and rejects Social Chapter of
Maastricht Treaty
Hypertext Markup Language (HTML) helps create the
World Wide Web
Hanif Kureishi: screenplays for *Sammy and Rosie Get Laid*
and *London Kills Me*
Pat Barker, *Regeneration*

1992   'Black Wednesday' stock market crisis when UK forced
to exit European Exchange Rate
Mechanism
Adam Thorpe, *Ulverton*

1993   Black teenager Stephen Lawrence murdered in Well Hall
Road, London
With Downing Street Declaration, PM John Major and
Taoiseach Albert Reynolds commit Britain and Ireland
to joint Northern Ireland resolution
Film of Ishiguro's *The Remains of the Day*, starring
Anthony Hopkins and Emma Thompson
Irvine Welsh, *Trainspotting*
Pat Barker, *The Eye in the Door*

1994   Tony Blair elected leader of Labour Party following
death of John Smith
Channel Tunnel opens
Nelson Mandela elected President of South Africa
Provisional IRA and loyalist paramilitary cease-fire
Homosexual age of consent for men in the UK
lowered to 18
Mike Newell (dir.), *Four Weddings and a Funeral*
Jonathan Coe, *What a Carve Up!*
James Kelman, *How Late It Was, How Late*, which wins
Booker Prize for Fiction
Irvine Welsh, *The Acid House*

1995   Oklahoma City bombing
Srebrenica massacre during Bosnian War
Pat Barker, *The Ghost Road*
Nicholas Hytner (dir.), *The Madness of King George*
Hanif Kureishi, *The Black Album*
Pat Barker, *The Ghost Road* (for which she is awarded the
Booker Prize for Fiction)

1996   Cases of Bovine Spongeiform Encephalitis (Mad Cow
Disease) in the UK
Divorce of Charles and Diana
Breaching cease-fire, Provisional IRA bombs London's
Canary Wharf and Central
Manchester
Film of Irvine Welsh's *Trainspotting* (dir. Danny Boyle),
starring Ewan McGregor and Robert Carlyle
Graham Swift, *Last Orders*, which wins Booker Prize

1997   Tony Blair becomes Labour PM after landslide victory
Princess Diana dies in Paris car crash
Hong Kong returned to China by UK
Jim Crace, *Quarantine*
Jonathan Coe, *The House of Sleep*, which wins Prix Médicis
Etranger (France)
Ian McEwan, *Enduring Love*
Iain Sinclair and Marc Atkins, *Lights Out for the Territory*

1998   Good Friday Agreement on Northern Ireland and
Northern Ireland Assembly established
Twenty-eight people killed by splinter group Real IRA
bombing in Omagh
Sonny Bono Act extends copyright to lifetime plus
70 years
BFI/Channel 4 film *Stella Does Tricks*, released (screenplay
A. L. Kennedy)
Julian Barnes, *England, England*
Pat Barker, *Another World*

1999   Euro currency adopted
Macpherson Inquiry into Stephen Lawrence murder
accuses London's Metropolitan Police of institutional
racism
NATO bombs Serbia over Kosovo crisis
Welsh Assembly and Scottish Parliament both open
Thirty-one passengers killed in Ladbroke Grove train
disaster

2000   Anti-globalization protest and riots in London
Hauliers and farmers blockade oil refineries in fuel price
protest in the UK
Kazuo Ishiguro, *When We Were Orphans*
Will Self, *How the Dead Live*
Zadie Smith, *White Teeth*

2001   9/11 Al-Qaeda attacks on World Trade Center and
Pentagon
Bombing and invasion of Afghanistan
Riots in Oldham, Leeds, Bradford and Burnley,
Northern England

Labour Party under Blair re-elected to government
Ian McEwan, *Atonement*
Pat Barker, *Border Crossing*

2002 Queen Mother dies aged 101
Rowan Williams named next Archbishop of Canterbury
Bali terrorist bomb kills 202 people and injures a
further 209
Inquiry concludes English general practitioner
Dr Harold Shipman killed around 215 patients
Slobodan Milosevic tried for genocide by the
International Criminal Tribunal for the Former
Yugoslavia in The Hague
Zadie Smith's *White Teeth* adapted for Channel 4
television broadcast in autumn

2003 Invasion of Iraq and fall of Saddam Hussein
Death of UK government scientist Dr David Kelly, and
Hutton Inquiry
Worldwide threat of Severe Acute Respiratory
Syndrome (SARS)
Pat Barker, *Double Vision*

2004 BBC Director General Greg Dyke steps down over Kelly
affair
Bombings in Madrid kill 190 people and injure over
1700
Expansion of NATO to include seven ex-Warsaw Pact
countries
European Union expands to 25 countries as eight
ex-communist states join
Jonathan Coe, *Like a Fiery Elephant: The Story of
B. S. Johnson*
Alan Hollinghurst, *The Line of Beauty*, which wins Booker
Prize for Fiction
Andrea Levy, *Small Island*, which wins Orange Prize for
Fiction

2005 UK ban on foxhunting with dogs comes into force
7/7 London suicide bombings on transport system kill

52 and injure over 700 commuters in morning rush
hour

Hurricane Katrina kills at least 1836 people and floods
devastate New Orleans

After four failed bombings are detected, Brazilian Jean
Charles de Menezes is shot and killed by Metropolitan
Police officers at Stockwell Underground Station

Ian McEwan, *Saturday*

Zadie Smith, *On Beauty*, which wins 2006 Orange Prize
for Fiction

2006   Jeanette Winterson awarded the OBE

Airline terror plot thwarted, causes major UK airline
delays

Israel–Hezbollah war in Lebanon

Five prostitutes killed in Ipswich in a six-week period

Saddam Hussein executed by hanging in controversial
circumstances

2007   Tony Blair stands down as Prime Minister to be replaced
by Gordon Brown

Pat Barker, *Life Class*

2008   Global Financial Crisis

Beijing Olympics

Barack Obama elected President of United States

2009   Global recession

Deaths of Henry Allingham, Harry Patch the last
surviving British veterans of the Great War

1

INTRODUCTION: WHY SHOULD WE READ PAT BARKER'S FICTION?

The novel as a genre has become progressively more up-to-date in its subject matter. In the opening lines of *Adam Bede* (1859), a landmark of English literary realism which concerns the lives of working-people, George Eliot attributes to the medium of ink a strange power of divination, strange because it was not a power of prevision and prophecy, but of retrospect, of 'far-reaching visions of the past' (Eliot, 5). Published in the year of Darwin's *Origin of Species*, Eliot's novel of ordinary, modern life was set during the wars against Napoleon, indeed in another century (1799). The fiction of our era can be more contemporary in its setting than Eliot's, though as the work of Pat Barker so strikingly illustrates, it may be historical fiction simultaneously. One way of answering the question why we should read Pat Barker's novels is to point to the way her novels seize on the contemporary, and in particular the ideas and values with which we inhabit our contemporary world, to provide far-reaching visions of the present. But to emphasize the novels' temporal relevance is to risk overlooking what makes these topical statements novels in the first place.

Franco Moretti, the most original student of the novel in our time, has suggested recently that the easily overlooked fact of the novel being in prose had two long-term stylistic consequences, which have bifurcated as the novel's low and high, its 'popular and cultivated' forms. On the one hand, prose is forward-looking, its meaning depending on what lies ahead, and so it generates the 'acceleration of narrative rhythm' characteristic of the novel about adventure (and the novel *as* an adventure). On the other hand, the subordination of clauses in the more 'continuous' constructions of prose yields complexity: 'the outcome is more than the sum of its parts, because subordination establishes a hierarchy among clauses, meaning becomes articulated, aspects emerge that didn't exist before' (Moretti, 112–13). Moretti's perspective on the 'uniquely adaptable and successful form of the novel' is geographical and demographic, and as the quotation suggests, it is also Darwinian. We are no longer talking about the *Rise of the Novel* but about the novel's variation, adaptation and evolution.

The two poles of style Moretti identifies can illuminate a single novel, or a single author's oeuvre, as well as the whole field of the novel. Pat Barker's fictions, it seems to me, reveal a characteristic interaction between acceleration and complexity, which becomes her signature. Barker creates and shapes characters, environments and stories which propel the reader forwards in quest of what happens next, of what is entailed. But this narrative momentum is refracted through forms and symbols which retard progress, detouring the reader into weighing alternative apprehensions of what is going on, to try out different ways of ordering complexity. Succession is continually mutating into contradiction, a then b into p and not-p. And the complexity is as compelling as the narrative propulsion.

One could come at these dimensions of Barker's fictional narratives in a slightly different way and recognize another signature of her work. The novels denote small worlds – a street, a hospital – but they connote or imply larger worlds. The local does not strain under the burden of representing the universal because Barker learned early on to make the specific, in particular a highly situated dialogue, the vehicle of the general. Her works are not novels of ideas, but ideas and the symbols which bear ideas are often as vividly present as her characters are. Philip Roth's fictional novelist Nathan Zuckerman describes the effects of the narratives of his hero E. I. Lonoff in terms which capture this quality very well:

> [they] produced ... the enigmatic reverberations of a gong, reverberations that left one wondering at how so much gravity and so

much levity could be joined, in so small a space, to a scepticism so
far-reaching.

(Roth, 20)

We should read Pat Barker's fiction because it makes us think as
it makes us feel, it causes us to stand back and ponder moral
and intellectual dilemmas at the same time as we are drawn into
identifying with her characters.

The author has recently described her career as 'odd . . . because
I appear to have changed sex in about 1986' (Garland, 185). As
well as indicating a significant shift in the subject matter of her
writing, this is a somewhat mischievous allusion to contemporary
fiction's internal ideological divisions, in particular the codifica-
tion of women's writing as discourse explicitly identified with
female writers, readers, characters or experience. The nuances of
these demarcations are lost in the folk-sociological and commercial coherence of the idea of gendered fiction in the UK market.
The notion of the 'Virago mandate' (Barker's first UK publisher
was a feminist imprint founded in 1973, which had become by the
end of that decade an important source of new writing by women
as well as a supplier of reprints of 'forgotten' novels) is another
signal of Barker's dissociation from feminist conceptions of both
authorship and readership. This will emerge as an important context for understanding the author's contemporaneity, particularly
the consonance of her themes with prominent discourses about
social and private life – for instance, our knowledge and practice
in relation to gender, social inequity and therapy – but also her distance from some of the progressive assumptions associated with
these discourses, such as feminism or welfarism.

Barker's apparent change of sex, the fact that her books in
the 1990s featured protagonists and settings (warriors and war)
which signalled participation in a conventionally masculine culture, correlated with developments in her handling of the historical past. Historical fiction has been transformed in the post-war
period by the way writers have exploited the porous and unstable
demarcation between fiction and non-fiction, stories and history.
No longer the elaboration of a fictional plot within an authen-
tic historical setting, 'historiographical metafiction', as the critic
Linda Hutcheon has dubbed the axiomatic postmodern form,
was the mutually reinforcing interplay of developments in the

self-referentiality of history and the novel. Increasingly sophisticated perceptions of the literary qualities of historical writing (notably Hayden White's insistence that narrative form transforms historical data) were interwoven with narrative styles which knowingly foregrounded storytelling and the properties of make-believe stories.

Contemporary fiction is historical because on one level there is no secure demarcation between factual and fictional stories. But on another level, history looms large because fictional stories are such a productive way of representing the contingency of the present, the dependence, that is, of our world and the entities which constitute it on earlier states of affairs. The Einsteinian revolutions in our comprehension of human life – the continuing impact of the theories of Darwin, Freud and Marx – all confer historical perspectives on those who have learned to think with them. Pat Barker's particular contribution to the contemporary historical novel is less a matter of metafictional narrative experiment than an engagement with the doubly contingent status of our historical consciousness. We understand and re-present the past in terms of concepts which are themselves historically contingent, shaped by our historical situation. We should read Pat Barker's fiction because, whether it is dramatizing the twentieth-century past or present, it embraces us in an examination of the meanings and values by which we live.

This is particularly apparent in Barker's Great War trilogy, which has ironically become a fixture in the reproduction of the literary myth which it set out to challenge. This has come about with the admission of *Regeneration* to the category of essential reading for the study of literary responses to 1914–18 at A level and on University courses. Barker has become a culturally central war writer by virtue of her fictional investigation of the meanings of war writing, rather than by virtue of her experience, a fact that breaks open the resistance of this otherwise positivistic literary field to the implications of the narrative constitution of fiction and non-fiction. An emphasis on war, however, is in danger of misrepresenting Pat Barker's writing, which is as much concerned with violence elsewhere than on the battlefield. Moreover, the trilogy is as interesting for what it shows us about the post-Cold War world in which it makes sense of the earlier war, as it is for its recreation of the early twentieth-century world of Home Front Britain.

The major arguments in this study can be understood as involving a historical appreciation of Barker's fiction. One concerns repetition, which is a return as well as a patterning overlaid on succession. That repetition is thematically central to the Freudian theories of dreams and war neurosis which the character Rivers adapts in his therapies in *Regeneration* suggests something of the potential richness of this idea within the worlds of Barker's books. But our main interest in repetition is formal, a question of how Barker's books are made as much as of what they are about. This encompasses the relationship of her writing to the work of other writers (e.g., canonical writers of the Great War). But it also invites a historical view of her oeuvre as a whole, when we consider her writing's relationship to itself, in particular the ways in which later books rewrite elements in earlier books. This is not a matter of disloyalty. Some writers write the same book over and over again: Jocelyn Brooke is an example of a writer who obeyed no formula but his own, and perhaps as a result was caught up in perfecting it. Barker's novels move the premises and the dramatis personae of their predecessors on in a forward development of their complexity, a renewal which is in part a dissatisfaction with a way of doing things, in part a discovery of new functions for an existing device. But there is also an element of repetition here, even of an unbeckoned return, or haunting. In answer to a question about being asked to talk about her characters as if they were real (the context was an encounter between novelists and psychotherapists), Barker stated:

> I'm in a difficult position because some of my characters are historical people so I can't just say, 'He did it because I made him do it.' ... I think of my characters as real people, and they come alive again when I talk about them in a rather destructive way, because they get in the way of the set of characters in the next book.
>
> (Garland, 199)

The voluntary and involuntary memories in her texts resonate with the theme of memory in her work. This theme manifests itself in many forms, from the dilemmas of personal identity to the 'sciences of memory'. The most important of Barker's forms is also explicitly connected with this field, in particular through the development of the device of fictional dialogue through an exploration of the particular verbal interactions of the psychoanalytic encounter. Academic interest in psychological trauma, a body of work which brings war and the psycho-analytic tradition into intimate connection at a moment when somatic wounds have virtually disappeared from the Western way of making and reporting war, is the most recent of the intellectual trends which Barker's work engages with. It remains a sceptical engagement.

> I think my work comes very close to therapy in that there is a preoc-cupation with darkness and trauma. But there is also a preoccupation about not letting that be the final word – by surrounding it with enough that is positive about life for it to take its place. And I think this must surely have a therapeutic equivalent. You don't want the client or the patient to ignore the traumatic event – you want them to remem-ber it. But equally you don't want to go to the other extreme so that the trauma becomes the truth about them, and the entire narrative of their life is the narrative of trauma. That is close to the balance I want to strike in my books.
>
> (Garland, 199)

That balance is located in the complexity of Barker's fiction, the way her storytelling holds dilemmas open even as her plots imply that for some characters at least there is a kind of resolution. And this is another reason why we should read her fiction, because it reminds us of the difference between the abstractions which com-pose our knowledge of ourselves in the world, and the intransigent particularity of experience.

PART II
Major Works

2

UNION STREET AND *BLOW YOUR HOUSE DOWN*

This chapter evaluates Barker's first two published novels, *Union Street* (1982) and *Blow Your House Down* (1984), stories about urban, working-class communities of women. Given that her later novels have a particular interest in masculinity, and become more and more concerned with middle-class lives, it might seem perverse to relate these early books to the rest of Barker's oeuvre in terms of a model of repetition rather than one of rejection or supercession. But ideas of return are a major thematic component of her books, most obviously in the therapeutic and historiographical aspects of her numerous renderings of the experience of the Great War. The novels are not only about repetition, they are acts of repetition in their own right. This latter attribute has two dimensions. One concerns Barker's allusiveness, her adaptations and borrowings. The other concerns her writing's relationship to itself, and in particular

the way later books reconfigure earlier ones (as will become apparent in the next chapter's account of what Barker has referred to as
her change of sex). Not only are these intertextual relationships
a significant effect in the style of Barker's early storytelling, they
also anticipate the developments of her later 1980s fiction prior to
what has come to be seen as her breakthrough book, *Regeneration*.

STREETWISE

Union Street is set in a Northern English town early in the last
quarter of the twentieth century. It is not explicitly a 1980s novel,
though the accident of its publication would help to focus attention on the book's potential function as an indictment of the
political ideology of Thatcherism as a cause of the further social
immiseration of economically marginal urban communities. The
title, *Union Street*, shares a punning ambivalence with the spray-
painted 'United' in Tony Harrison's miners' strike poem V (1985,
broadcast 1987): union in both works connotes marriage, community and the organization of labour. These ideals and institutions are travestied by the circumstances Barker narrates, but they
can still function locally to belie both the apparent necessity of
human misery and the artistic inevitability of an ironic assessment
of human potential.

Union Street is constructed from seven narratives, each named
after a female protagonist, ranging from just-teenage Kelly Brown
to the 76-year-old Alice Bell. Indeed, the relationship between the
generations represented by these women is more significant than
the precise historical setting of the narrative's present. The reader
is challenged to decode the temporality of the street rather than
recognize narrative references to the headline events of a public chronicle. For instance, the miners' strike referred to in 'Kelly
Brown' alludes to the conditions of the early 1970s, to the political and economic power of the unions during the premiership of
Ted Heath, to the 'winter of discontent' and the three-day week,
but this kind of cross-referencing is less important than it will be
in *Liza's England*.

In the seven ages of woman Barker tacitly acknowledges
Shakespeare's Jaques, in *As You Like It*, for whom persons are
'merely players' on the world's stage, their 'acts being seven ages'
(2.7.140–3). The novel lines up with a tradition of revisionist

narratives which substitute for the schoolboy, soldier and justice of Jaques' collective and normative biography of man the
unrecorded lives of women. This politicized rewriting is associated in particular with the fictional practice and the feminist
polemic of Virginia Woolf between the wars. The allusions are
a cue to the reader to start making sense of the diachronic or
historical patterns in the lives which are opened to view by the narrative's synchronic snap-shots of female experience. It also points
us, ironically, to all that divides the individuals who live cheek by
jowl in the street – repeating each other's experiences – divides
them both from each other, and from their own pasts and futures.
Comparison has been drawn with James Joyce's *Dubliners* (1914)
in which stories are similarly sequenced in the order of the protagonists' ages, and in which the younger characters intuit failed
futures in the ruin of their seniors (Brannigan in Monteith et al.,
2005, 10). But where Joyce's characters remain largely immune to
each other's predicaments (and to Joyce's capacity to recognize
them), Barker shares the saving power of irony with her characters, and permits them an occasional transcendence of their
temporarily fixed position in a world of evolving desire and experience. This is a device which charges the naturalistic or sociological objectivity of the novel's unidealizing narrative with the shock
of the painfully un-deluded.

The formal as well as the thematic (especially social and
familial) relationships the novelist creates among her characters
combine to emphasize questions about both biological and socio-
economic determination – or destiny – in the lives of the women
of Union Street. The material environment is itself precarious,
and not the constant that the localized cycle of generational
repetition might imply. The shaping of the stories into a larger
structure promises to align the several 'lives' or narratives in an
overarching interpretation of the conditions in which individuals struggle to flourish, an interpretation which goes beyond the
immediately obvious colouring of the novel through its episodes
of rape, domestic violence, desertion, bereavement, family break-
up and death. The gender of the author and her protagonists,
together with the Virago imprint, assign the novel to the category of women's fiction, or, as Justine Picardie put it in a review of
Regeneration, 'the ghetto of women's writing' (Westeman, 63). This
generates further expectations that the significance the novel gives

to its constituent stories will be broadly feminist, involving a critique of the way life is organized to prioritize the interests of men as well as positive representations of women's experience. Judging how far Barker works within or against these emergent generic parameters will be important in reading her early fiction, and also in understanding how her fiction develops into the 1990s.

Given the importance of age to the structure of *Union Street*, it is striking how much trouble we have in settling the question of just how old is the protagonist of the first story Kelly Brown – 'It's not as if she was old-looking for her age' (37). Her experience is at odds with the categories we might think it appropriate to apply to her: as the Governess claims of the supposedly possessed Flora in Henry James's *The Turn of the Screw* (1898), 'at such times she's not a child: she's an old, old woman' (James, 66). Our notions of Kelly's possession – the extent to which she has been possessed by others, and is possessed of herself – influence the background assumptions we make about her age, as we figure out the implications of the way she is perceived within her improvised family, as well as by sexual predators. The novel draws forth the reader's prejudgements and prejudices in order to confront them. This further reveals how strongly Barker's writing about working-class women is rooted in a scenic technique which plays down the authority of the third-person narrator, and in the figurative rather than denotative dimension of style.

Our reading of Kelly's age is of course bound up with the violence which divides her from her childhood: the novel plays on residual cultural idealizations of the long childhood which have survived both the Freudian revolution, and the superficial rejection of bourgeois Victorian ideologies. These idealizations also survive their contradiction, in the later twentieth century, by the economic prerogatives of families living in poverty. Barker anticipates Kelly's rape with a conceit on the girl's pastime of conkering:

> She watched his long fingers with their curved nails probe the green skin, searching for the place where it would most easily open and admit them.
>   . . . .
> When she looked back he had got the conker open. Through the gash in the green skin she could see the white seed.
> 'No, you were right,' he said. 'It's not ready yet.'

> He threw it away and wiped his fingers very carefully and fastidi-
> ously on his handkerchief, as if they were more soiled than they could
> possibly have been.
>
> (*Union Street*, 14)

There is a certain fastidiousness about this proleptic enactment
of violation and its aftermath. The conceit initially appears exor-
bitant in its spelling out of a likeness between fruit and sexual
parts, from the cutting of an opening and the greenness of the
object, to the perpetrator's dissociation from his act. But the effect
is the antithesis of the pastoral simplification often suggested by
a botanical analogy. This is a disturbing piece of writing – the
fairytale horror of the knife-like fingers, the suggestion of the
slang sense of 'gash' (vulva) which contributes to the story's strin-
gent appraisal of the adequacy of the language of both fiction
and report for telling what happens to Kelly. A similar effect is
generated by the extended allusion to W. B. Yeats's 'Leda and
the Swan', the poet's version of the myth of Zeus's rape of Leda
(which engenders Helen whose beauty 'caused' the Trojan War).
The geese which Kelly feeds in the park metamorphose into Yeats's
phallic swan:

> She looked down at the mottled flesh of her thighs and remembered
> how the yellow beaks had jabbed. Then up at him. All her original
> distrust had returned.

The allusion is signalled both by verbal coincidence with Yeats's
sonnet – beak, thighs – and by ironic incongruence:

> Did she put on his knowledge with his power
> Before the indifferent beak could let her drop?
>
> (Yeats, 322)

The transference of power in 'Kelly Brown' however is no apotheo-
sis, but a traumatic entry into adulthood, and a change of identity:
Kelly '*was* what had just happened to her' (32).

The novel does not assert a straightforward relationship
between Kelly's rape and her social environment, nor make her
story symbolize women's experience. She is mute for 3 weeks
(the rapist's pursuit is reprised 'down the howling corridors of

nightmares', the first of Barker's devices to register trauma). Then, repeating the symbol of the cleaved conker, Kelly's voice returns:

> with a sensation of splitting open, of pissing on the floor, she started to scream.
>
> They came. They sat over her. But the feeling of numbness was back. She tried to tell them about his face. She tried to tell them about that moment in the fish and chip shop when the grown-up man had started to cry. But they weren't interested in that. They wanted her to tell them what had happened in the alley behind the boarded-up factory. And they wanted her to tell it again and again and again. (57–8)

The forensic reiteration of 'what happened' is a reduction of the rape to the biomechanical ('he stuck it all the way in'), and one that is repeated in the novel's leitmotif of mechanical 'piston-like' intercourse (62). Barker's own storytelling is the antithesis of the story the authorities want to hear. Some of the narrative devices in 'Kelly Brown' work to impede the objectification of the rape which occurs in the socially coded roles and actions of the rapist and the victim. Explored at greater length in *Blow Your House Down*, the public labelling of violence against women is represented here either as denial ('they behaved as if the child had been ill') or vigilantism, the latter re-enacting the performance of masculine power, as in the 'civic zeal' of Mr Broadbent, roused by his indignation at sexual offenders to copulate on, rather than with, his wife (45–6).

The writing of 'Kelly Brown' elicits other, more ambivalent responses to violation. One involves Kelly's family, her position in it as youngest child and the absent father whom she seeks in her attacker (feeding the geese is what daughters do with their dads). Mrs Brown, too, in a 'spasm of hatred', identifies her long-gone husband with 'The Man' (35; *The Man Who Wasn't There* will later revisit both themes). Kelly sees the Man's post-rape fear in the cracking face of her mother as she loses control (59): thus the narrative closes the distance between Kelly's projection of a desire for a father figure, and her mother's distrust of men. It also unhinges assumptions about the content and meaning of childhood. We are prompted to calibrate Kelly's naivety (what we might call her innocence) by the terms she draws on to make sense of the rape: 'half-understood jokes' about male sexual potency, lavatory graffiti and memories of 'other confrontations, with teachers or policemen' (32, 28). Yet the rape transforms her in her mother's eyes into a repellent maturity, promoting her to the status her elder sister has already assumed as a sexual rival in relation to the transient 'uncles' who have taken the place of the father. From this (misogynist) perspective, innocence becomes a culpable or flirtatious naivety about the (natural and inevitable) behaviour of men.

Despite the wealth of allusive and figurative devices which point up its literariness, *Union Street* has acquired something of a documentary status: twenty years ago, Lyn Pykett noted this by quoting novelist Doris Lessing's view that 'we read novels for information about areas of life we don't know' (Pykett, 74). Indeed, the sociological ambitions of the nineteenth-century literary realism associated with the French novelist Balzac, who flattered the readers of his *Père Goriot* (1835) with the assertion that only Parisians would understand its presentation of Paris, is brought to mind by an idea Barker attributes to Iris King: 'Nobody who hadn't lived there could understand' (187). But this scepticism about the possibility of vicarious knowledge (which is also associated with current arguments about the possibility of representing atrocity and the violence of war) is one reason why the novel does not confine itself to a positivistic, documentary register. As Ian Haywood notes, Barker is 'reinventing old social territory' (Haywood, 145). For instance, Barker devises surreal juxtapositions in her account of the everyday. Kelly's newly apparent sexual precocity (the status the rape confers on her in the eyes of others – 'his eyes created her') is signalled by the visibility of her nipples, 'like eyes in her chest' (*US*, 16, 43). The linkage of sexuality and the visual field, drawing on the visual repertoire of European surrealism (e.g., an inversion of René Magritte's 'Le Viol' of 1934), aligns the novel with the concept of the male gaze, a theoretical term (developed by Laura Mulvey in the 1970s) for the way that film and the visual arts construct and reproduce normative apperceptions of women for both men and women. 'You couldn't avoid seeing them'; Kelly's pubescence recruits her into a symbolic order which unfailingly reproduces misogynist codings of the body, for instance her 'grubbiness . . . was no longer childish dirt. It looked sluttish' (43). The male characters in *Union Street* are both pathetic and terrible, superfluous and indispensable, materially absent and ideologically omnipotent; their misogyny is lodged in the interactions of the women of Union Street, in particular their way of looking at each other (structurally crucial to the novel's interlinking of storylines): 'every older woman became an image of the future, a reason for hope or fear' (94).

The surreal is an instance of the transgression of normative schema or concepts. Barker confronts her readership with matter over which polite culture (perhaps now better described as panic culture) draws a veil – for instance violence inflicted on children and women, the body and its fluids, and sexual behaviours – and clearly there is an intention to shock. This is not, as we will see in *Blow Your House Down*, simply a matter of inclusivity with respect to novelistic fiction's referential or denotative functions. The way Barker forms these episodes linguistically and figuratively suggests a determination to go beyond the canons of positivist realism in narrating twentieth-century lives. Surrealism has it origins in the idea of dream writing, an expression of what André Breton called 'the real functioning of the mind'. Barker employs devices which recall surrealist 'psychic automatism' to colour the novel's rendering of external world with the polymorphousness of conscious and unconscious states.

Kelly herself comes to identify with the Man, with predation: 'the real defence was to be one of those who leapt,' a resonance amplified by the ambiguous recurrence of an image of a British soldier in Belfast (4, 47). But the chapter counteracts this identification thematically through the sympathy elicited in Kelly by the figure of the old woman, the 'heap of old rags' (66). In formal terms, the first section of the novel is linked with the last (we will recognize Alice Bell as the old woman on the bench when the encounter is repeated in the seventh part). At the novel's end Kelly's discovery that 'an old woman had once been a child' (specifically her acquisition of a belief in mortality) is dramatized in Alice's memorial preparations for death (67). Kelly's hungry stare after the women leaving work at the bakery (a falling into step homewards, and a kind of reintegration with the feminine after her phallic, piston-like walking of the streets) is also a bridge into the second part, whose subject, Joanne Wilson, is seen by Kelly lingering at the factory gate to meet her boyfriend.

Pregnant Joanne regards the physical signs of maternity with fear; her body has become strange to her 'like another face, with nipples instead of eyes' (72). The iconographic echo of Kelly's disquieting pubescence, and the violent cancellation of her childhood, demands reflection on the relationship between rape and the dating couple's 'negotiations' over premarital sexual activity. Iris King drills into her girls the literal penalty of sexual relations with feckless men: 'Sixteen years. They don't do as much as that for murder' (201). Joanne's boyfriend Ken greets news of his baby by 'trying to screw it out of her', mechanical thrusting turned into an instrument of abortion. Prenatal termination is a figure for terminated dreams, even as abortion (say in the case of Brenda King) is resorted to in the belief that those dreams can be sustained a while longer. This applies to the realm of labour, as well as to maternity: on the production-line of the bakery '[e]ach half-formed thought was aborted by the arrival of another cake' (85). Even fantasy is subdued to the rhythms of work. Iris, a proletarian version of Virginia Woolf's Mrs Dalloway – 'she loved life' – nevertheless procures an abortion for her daughter. Images of aborted foetuses – her stillborn first child, Brenda's live-born child left, 'red as raw meat', to die on the floor of the lavatory – haunt her pleasure in the married daughter and (male) grandchild she hopes will escape the cycle of poverty and violence. Kelly, who finds Brenda's baby amidst the rubble of demolition, guards the secret of its burial 'as if it had been her own', ritually re-enacting the burial of her own childhood (62).

The women of *Union Street* are never relieved of paid and unpaid work; even Blonde Dinah, taken by retired George Harrison to be the same age as his wife, is still seeking trade as a prostitute. But the men are out of work, and alternately diminished or puffed up in violent self-assertion as a consequence. Lisa Goddard's husband Brian beats her and squanders her savings. John Scaife's respiratory illness is either an occupational hazard or an ingrained malingering only work will cure. His invalidism is also symptomatic of his cultural alienation from his grammar-school-educated son. The scene of wife Muriel's tending her haemorrhaging husband will be repeated in *Liza's England*, transformed into a more extended meditation on the father–son relationship tangentially addressed here, a repetition which is a significant episode in Barker's disavowal of the gendered generic framework she'd worked within in the early novels.

The redundancy of the novel's men is strongly determined by socio-economic factors (industrial decline, structural unemployment) but the women's lives are plotted on a cycle of reproduction. As we have seen this can be aborted, but it is stronger even than the misogynist devaluation of the girl child: 'Don't bring it round here if it's got a crack in it' (135). Liza Goddard is frightened by blood in her daughter's nappy; in a sense she misreads the nature of the curse, which is not disease but the fertility prefigured in this neonatal 'first period' (137). But she comes to recognize just this, recalling bird-nesting expeditions that resulted in 'orgies of destruction': 'the thought that inside that tiny body was a womb like hers with eggs waiting to be released, caused the same fear, the same wonder' (138–9).

This mystery of creation is reprised in the scene where George Harrison examines the body of the sleeping Dinah, seeing for the first time 'A gash? A wound? Red fruit bitten to the core? It was impossible to say what it was like' (231). Barker's version of Gustave Courbet's scandalous and long-secreted painting 'The Origin of the World' (1866) is a canny image of the sequestration of life by the powerful. Harrison's post-coital jauntiness, back to his old self, depends on burying the shame of his relation to Dinah.

The dignity which the prostitute is necessarily denied so that her clients may expel their guilt through projection is the social counterpart to the unyielding force of biological reproduction; in the person of Iris King or Alice Bell reputation is more than keeping up appearances, it is a perpetual struggle to shore up an autonomy in defiance of the depredations of an economic system predicated on the perpetuation of poverty, the humiliations of domination by weak but dangerous men, and the unending process by which families beget new families. Sustaining life materially and culturally is a constant labour; reproducing life appears by contrast a momentary and happy accident, which nevertheless renews the burden. The pathetic injustice of the contradictions which arise from this asymmetry is testimony to an undiminished core of identity: Iris holding the family together by hiding her father's beatings from the 'cruelty police', Alice losing ground economically across the decades since the Slump. This theme might suggest an idealization of urban, working-class motherhood in a legend of indomitable care, but there is little else in the novel to commend this reading. In the case of Alice Bell, who, fearing the workhouse, runs from the prospect of a convalescent home to become an internal refugee like Kelly, dying with dignity means reassembling the fragments, the rubbish (gash) which her failing health is turning her into, and resisting the doctor's examination, which has taught her 'the indignity of rape' (260). The chapter is an inversion of Tolstoy's *The Death of Ivan Ilyich* (1886), familial neglect leading not to self-accusation but self-affirmation, notably in terms of motherhood, of acting as a relay in the reproduction of life. The closing paragraphs, in which is attempted a mode of transcendence that the foregoing pages have strenuously discounted, redeploy the imagery of dark and light which Tolstoy had used to imagine what dying was like; in Barker's case to frame the closing of circles in the joined hands of old woman and girl. The motif is reprised in the spiralling of swooping birds, an image that strongly recalls the way another linguistically distinctive novel of proletarian life, Henry Green's factory novel *Living* (1929), resolves on pigeons lifting in flight from the hood of a pram. The spirals are definitely not Yeatsian gyres, metaphysical forms with which to bring order to mundane experience: putting Kelly on the last page is about as effective a way as can be imagined of aborting a transcendent impulse.

PORNOGRAPHY: *BLOW YOUR HOUSE DOWN* AND THE YORKSHIRE RIPPER CASE

> Jack the Ripper who sits at the head of the chamber of commerce.
>
> (Dylan, 'Tombstone Blues')

> It gives life and humanity back to the working-class women – prostitutes or not – and some working-class men too, whom the 'Ripper case' had taken it away from.
>
> (Jouve, 144)

My use of the term pornography is intended to draw attention to what is really at stake in *Blow Your House Down* (1984), a novel whose *dramatis personae* consists of whores and punters. Although Barker has insisted in interview that she was not writing about the Yorkshire Ripper (Nixon, 15), this narrative is notable for being her first in which a historical figure has invaded the fictional frame.

The reader's associations between Peter Sutcliffe (born 1946, criminally active 1975–81) and the 'Ripper' who kills two of Barker's characters and attacks another foreshadows aspects of the reincarnation of the famous Wilfred Owen in *Regeneration*. The narrative also assumes the point of the view of the 'Ripper' in an important but repellent scene. This character anticipates Barker's version of Owen most pertinently in being (in excess of material facts) a mythic actor in a realm of violence which haunts 'normal' society, a realm invariably represented as at once alien and familiar.

The serial killer has been described by a North American commentator as 'a romantic icon, like the cowboy' (Joel Achenbach, quoted in Jenkins, 3). Modern Britain supplies no such ready counterpart, but there are intersections between the ways our national culture cultivates a fascination with, respectively, criminal and military killers, and with the landscapes in which their victims are displayed. (This is most notable in the 'Yorkshire noir' quartet of novels by David Peace, a sequence of stylistically experimental crime thrillers which recycle a period setting.) Barker's writing brings this congruence to our attention, inviting us to reflect on the heroes and villains of the various kinds of stories we tell about violence both out there in the world and within ourselves.

The word 'pornography' is a nineteenth-century compound-formation from Greek roots and it refers to the 'description of the life, manners, etc., of prostitutes and their patrons'. Eighteenth-century English literature provides well-known examples of such descriptions: Daniel Defoe's *Roxana* (1724) and John Cleland's *Fanny Hill* (1748–49) are still in print as Penguin Classics. Indeed, the rise of the novel as a genre of English literary writing has, in this sense, a significant pornographic dimension. But the term as it was deployed a century later additionally signified an evaluation of such material viewed as 'the expression or suggestion of obscene or unchaste subjects in literature or art' (*OED*). The history of the word 'pornography' reflects the degree to which nineteenth-century English culture was concerned with the dissemination and control of such images. The word had immediate application to both the culture of antiquity (e.g., wall paintings unearthed at Pompeii) and the 'obscene or unchaste' in contemporary discourse or imagery. Dunglison's *Medical Lexicon* provides an early example of the public interest defence for attention to the proscribed, defining pornography as 'a description of prostitutes or of prostitution, as a matter of public hygiene'. The seventh edition, from which the citation is taken, appeared in 1857, the year of the Obscene Publications Act which warranted the seizure of obscene materials, the legal 'test' for which was defined in 1868, in *Queen v. Hicking*, as 'the tendency . . . to deprave and corrupt' (Wilson, 142). The test of pornography was its effects on its audience (a view which the New Critical school of modern literary criticism would call the 'affective fallacy', or the mistaking of the reader's impressions for the text which brought that effect into being).

One hundred years later, a new Obscene Publications Act (1959) persisted in the affective definition of pornography even as it outlined a 'defence of public good allowing for evidence of artistic, literary or scientific merit', that is, exceptions on the basis of an elevation to the category of the supposedly non-instrumental aesthetic (Williams Report 1979, quoted in Wilson, 143). This understanding of pornography in terms of reception was renewed in the succeeding era of liberalization – an era characterized by a commercial/technological formation (notably Video) in which pornography entered the economic if not the cultural mainstream – but in the form of a broadly feminist critique of pornography as a primer for male violence against women (Itzin, passim). The continuity from The Vice Society to Women Against Violence Against Women is a striking one, as Blake Morrison suggested in his vision of an alliance between the reactionary clean-up-TV-campaign of Mary Whitehouse and the radicalism of populist–feminist Germaine Greer (Morrison, 1998, 216).

This is the context within which Pat Barker's execution of pornography (a writing which is about prostitutes, and not per se a writing which corrupts) confronts us with both the sociological and affective dimensions of the representation of power and sexuality. It is worth noting, too, in anticipation of the claims that Barker's fiction is too derivative of influential academic scholarship. In this instance Barker's presentation of a cultural fetish in the making – the Yorkshire Ripper – can be juxtaposed with a strong, theoretical reading of the phenomenon which appeared 2 years later, Nicole Ward Jouve's *'The Streetcleaner': The Yorkshire Ripper Case on Trial* (1986).

Jouve's reading of the Ripper investigation and trial is notable for its analysis of the construction of Sutcliffe's victims as a foil for the projections out of which the police and the press created the figure of the 'Ripper'. The following passage, which occurs two-thirds of the way through the book, is not typical of Jouve's analytic register, with its conceptual sources in feminism, semiotics and psychoanalysis, but it offers a significant evaluation of Barker's novel as a critique of the cultural reproduction of violent patriarchy:

> To get a balanced picture, the story of the victims should also be told. The story of the loving home of Jayne MacDonald, whose father died of grief. The story of Emily Jackson, who went in for prostitution because she *liked* it – no doubt the money was handy too; it also took her mind off the acute pain caused by the death of one of her children. But the easy-going tolerance of her husband, and her own love for her children – like the love of Wilma McCann and Jean Jordan and others for theirs – should be celebrated. As should the heroism of Olive Smelt, who took a job in an old men's home to try and cure herself of the aversion to men her bludgeoning left her scarred with. There is perhaps more *real* courage in such deeds than in the heady storming of enemy positions: Victoria Crosses don't go to the right quarters.
>
> Fiction is probably the only way in which such a celebration could occur. The victims have been hurt too badly not to be spared the limelight of any further discussion. Pat Barker's remarkable novel, *Blow Your House Down*, is the fictional answer. It gives life and humanity back to the working-class women – prostitutes or not – and some working-class men too, whom the 'Ripper case' had taken it away from.
>
> (Jouve, 144)

Blow Your House Down in this view becomes a kind of reparation – in the absence of Victoria Crosses (*Regeneration* will begin with Sassoon throwing away his medal ribbon). This reparation must be enacted in the field of make-believe ('fictional') because the real victims have already suffered at the hands of a regime of representation. Barker's pornography in this argument is an extended counter-statement, a voicing of what is silenced, and a scrupulous revision of a dismissive or exploitative misrepresentation of prostitutes. In Jouve's reading of the Ripper case, it was as if Sutcliffe, the self-styled 'Streetcleaner', 'was on the side of society' (27). The way the murders and murderer were described and explained leads her to analyze the parallels between Sutcliffe's revulsion at the feminine (labelling all women as prostitutes by killing them) and the subordination of women in a society in which men are schooled in 'institutionalized violence' (153). If the threat of the Ripper led to the revival of certain forms of social segregation (the focus of reclaim-the-night demonstrations), the discursive construction of this figure as menace and celebrity reinforced normal or invisible exclusions of women from 'humanity' (Jouve employs the very same term – 'humanity', in practice an exclusionary pseudo-universal – as did the Nigerian novelist Chinua Achebe in analysing the teaching of Conrad's *Heart of Darkness* in US universities as a masking of racism).

But *Blow Your House Down* has been found wanting precisely because it is pornographic, that is, a rendition of the figure of the prostitute. Angela McRobbie's pessimism about Barker's project appears all the more authoritative for its cosmopolitan, non-Yorkshire, context:

> What more can be done with the image of the prostitute? From Walter Benjamin to Martin Scorcese she has been a figure who represents a challenge to the hypocrisies of conventional sexual morality, but *always* she is punished: possibly because she also challenges the men themselves. (25)

Barker will quite specifically qualify the categorical nature of this claim, both endorsing and modifying it, by staging a discussion of Oscar Wilde's scandalous play *Salome*, in *The Eye in the Door* (156–7). But *Blow Your House Down* had already tested the possibility of a writing of prostitutes that does not contribute to violence against women, and representations of 'obscene and unchaste' subjects which do not 'deprave and corrupt'. Indeed, we could call it a critical pornography, following Angela Carter's notion of how 'a moral pornographer might use pornography as a critique of current relations between the sexes' (Carter, 19).

Barker's critique is bound up with her writing's ambiguous relationship to an aesthetics of confrontation. When Barker springs these encounters on us (largely in the field of sexuality and violence, and often involving a rather stylish taboo-breaking), she appears to share war-photographer Don McCullin's intent to 'break the hearts and spirits of secure people' (McCullin, 172). This is made the explicit theme of *Double Vision*, which weaves atrocity journalism and Goya into its narrative about the relations of

English security and both international and English aggro. The epigraph of *Blow Your House Down*, drawn from the philosopher Friedrich Nietzsche's 1886 text *Beyond Good and Evil* (§ 146), underlines the author's determination that as her readers we should look on that from which we might prefer to avert our eyes:

> Whoever fights monsters should see to it that in the process he does not become a monster. And when you look long into an abyss the abyss also looks into you.
>
> (Nietzsche, 1973, 84)

The first sentence has a rather mechanical application to Barker's plot: the monster is the 'Ripper'; the one who fights him is Jean. She is a prostitute whose mission to make the streets safe is narrated in the first-person in the third section of the novel: she takes over from the police who use prostitutes as bait, and who might otherwise appear to be allies of the 'streetcleaner' figure. Convinced she has snared the 'Ripper', she fatally stabs a punter. The second sentence has a more complicated relationship to the novel and our reading of it. Ostensibly, the abyss is represented by the trauma of Maggie, a survivor of a 'Ripper' attack who is posited 'trying to come back' (like Nicole Ward Jouve's unacknowledged female heroes). Jouve herself cites this word, abyss, as Barker's, but glosses Nietzsche's dialectic when she writes of her own nightmares at the time of the Ripper trial: 'I could not stop him . . . from looking at me'. That look carries the power of definition: the monster's gaze turns the victim into a monster, that is, a prostitute ('I had experienced the guilt there was in being a woman . . . . What would happen if I put myself forward to be seen, joined the side of prostitution?' (Jouve, 27)).

The epigraph, taken as a whole, signals a double-bind: Barker's prostitutes can escape neither the monstrosity to which they are condemned by the 'Ripper's' crimes and the police investigation, nor the logic which puts them outside the law if they attempt to circumvent the criminological nexus. For the reader Barker has created a perspective of the abyss in the abomination of an impersonation of the 'Ripper', shifting focalization from prostitute/victim to punter/murderer, and narrating rape and slaughter from his point of view. This is controversial because art itself is complicit in violence. As Nietzsche has it in *The Birth of*

Tragedy (1872), Apollonian culture (founded in principles of order and control) must always 'slay monsters' and 'through its potent dazzling representations and its pleasurable illusions, must have triumphed over a terrible depth of world-contemplation and a most keen sensitivity to suffering' (Nietzsche, 1995, 9).

The episode is notable for its elaboration of the specific actions that are compounded into the 'Ripper's' killing. Readers made uncomfortable by the alignment with the aggressor are pushed to assess whether this unease is visceral or theoretical. Barker's descriptions are a vehicle for speculating about the 'Ripper's' psychology or interiority, a device often associated with affirmation or the generation of sympathy in narrative fiction, though Austrian nobel-laureate Elfriede Jelinek's novel *Greed* (2000, trans. 2007) is an example of a text which utterly undermines this effect. More troublingly, the male agent's impotence impedes any desire the reader might have to move swiftly through and past the dynamic phase of violence to its conclusion in a stasis which may be consolatory. The confusion of 'The sleeping and the dead' (66) is of course an ironic figure at the heart of Wilfred Owen's writing, a by-now traditional way of signifying the ironic apperceptions with which we shield ourselves from the violence of war (as opposed to its productive functions). But the rhythm of the episode is a sequence of frustrations which elicit more violence. The 'Ripper' character is determined to '*make* himself come', but the prostitute Kath is drunk and her giggles undermine his performance. He begins to 'slide ignominiously out' but derives satisfaction from her 'squeal of pain'. He is further excited by his attempt to sodomize Kath, to force 'a way into her darkness'. When the thrusts of his penis miss their target, he hits her. As she moves to accommodate him, he exults '*you filthy cow*' (i.e., redescribing his violence as feminine wantonness). But his penis 'felt small'; he examines it and at first it looks 'as usual' (imperial purple) but then he notices 'a drop of gingery fluid'. He lashes out at the smell and sight of her faeces, with fists and then a knife. 'At some point, unnoticed by him, Kath died.'

> After a few minutes he was able to stop and look down. It wasn't enough that she was dead, he needed more. He gathered handfuls of feathers together and started shoving them inside her cunt. It wasn't easy: as fast as he pushed them inside they turned red. He had to

practically stuff her with them, like stuffing a chicken, before he could get the effect he wanted: a ridiculous little white frill between her legs. (65)

There is evidence that Barker's device – both for its deliberate confusion of the sexual and of violence, and its alignment of the reader with the perpetrator – is disconcerting.

British academics seem loathe to cite or analyze this example of Barker's motivation of conventionally obscene words, contexts and actions, and invariably approach Kath's rape via the text's reiterated parallels with the production line in the chicken factory, even as that same symbolic apparatus is denigrated as 'somewhat heavy' (Palmer, 89; Childs, 67–8). A creaking symbolic structure is clearly preferable to looking 'into the abyss' (Joannou, 45–6). Sarah Daniels's 1995 stage adaptation replaced the 'Ripper' and his script with the figure of 'The Chicken Man', who takes Polaroids of the carcass he stuffs with its own feathers, a revision that only underlines the controversial impact of Barker's impersonation (Bartleet, 89–90). A North-American academic who has put herself on record urging her students to record their disquiet at the novel, rather than rehearsing 'politically correct pronouncements on class and gender oppression', nevertheless observes that these same students 'note, rightly I think, that Kath's murder is pornographic, in the sense that Barker shows the murderer's association of sex and violence without reassuring us that we are being offered a critique of this behaviour' (Ardis, 20). This disturbance derives from the convergence of narrative and the pathological in Barker's composition. As Mark Seltzer explains, in his analysis of the naming event which gave rise to the term 'serial killer' in the 1970s, the label really captured 'the internal competition between repetition and representation':

> the real meaning of serial killing is a failed series of attempts to make the scene of the crime equivalent to the scene of the fantasy – that is ... a failed series of attempts to make the content of the act and the fantasy of the actor, act and motive, perfectly coincide.
>
> (Seltzer, 64)

The narration of the murder of Kath (which has its own repetitions in the novel) is offensive precisely because it activates these analogies through manipulation of point of view in what *The Eye in the Door* will call 'a meshing together of fantasies' (*Eye*, 52).

These anxieties about reading pornography, and the problems critics have in squarely facing Barker's citation and creation of obscenity, confirm the ambivalence in Barker's investment in cultural icons of horror. On the one hand, we might worry whether Barker's fiction is a species of titillation; on the other, we might be tempted to join Peter Childs in describing her particular renditions of violence as an effort to 'reverse the desensitizing effects of over-familiarity on our responses to violence and its effects' (69). But Nicole Ward Jouve's commentary on obscenity and the Ripper case provides another framework for thinking through the nature of our responses to literary abomination.

> Sutcliffe's victims were *not* 'obscene'. He inscribed obscenity upon them . . . by displaying them and wounding them in such a way as to make them legible as such. By defacing them, 'labouring' at them with tools which industry uses to mould and subdue nature, he was placing them outside culture, outside the walls of the city . . . . Stuffed under an old sofa, in a piece of wasteground, horsehair pushed into her mouth, her poor body battered by a lump-hammer, left to rot undiscovered for a month, Yvonne Pearson could indeed appear like Abomination, the 'plague' upon the city. No human being would want to identify with her.
>
> The trouble was that Sutcliffe's *text* was read as he meant it to be read. All the accounts I have seen of the discovery of the bodies of his victims insist upon the horror of the 'sight' he had left. 'It made even hardened detectives blanch' . . . . About Yvonne Pearson, Cross's comment is [quoting *The Yorkshire Ripper: The In-depth Study of a Mass Killer and His Methods* (Granada, 1981)]: 'it was a humiliating end for a girl who saw herself as a cut above many of her fellow prostitutes.' . . . That one feel grief, or pity, or any of the fellow-feeling that would go to the victims of a terrorist massacre, does not even seem to be envisaged. (165–6)

Barker ensures that her 'Ripper' doesn't, as she puts it, 'get the effect he wanted' (65). The scene of Kath's rape, murder and mutilation is closed with two paragraphs in the third-person, together with second-person conditionals: 'If you approached the mattress casually you would see nothing but a heap of old rags. You would tread on her before you realized a woman's body lay there.'

The narrator's speculation about our hypothetical response to the content of the scene (but not its form) is pitched somewhere between the shared intuition of pathos in impoverishment and diminution (like the febrile Gervaise stuffed in the cupboard under the stairs in Zola's *L'Assommoir*, 1876–77) and a charge of not recognising the victim, of dehumanizing her. The presence of this device does not, however, resolve the question of how we might be implicated in a culture of normalized violence through our reading of the text of Barker's 'Ripper'.

Another measure of what Barker does in the novel is by comparison with other literary treatments of the Yorkshire Ripper phenomenon. Blake Morrison's revival of the ballad form to tell a story about Sutcliffe provides an immediate contrast with the devices of *Blow Your House Down*. Its single narrative voice belongs to the Ripper's peer group, though the balladeer's explanation of the Ripper's motives requires a division from that group's ideal of masculinity:

> No, Pete weren't drove by vengeance,
> Roundtwistedness or ale,
> But to show isen a baufy man (Morrison, 1985, 9)

'The Ballad of the Yorkshire Ripper' has a circular structure, with the addition that the reprise of the opening verses resolves on the balladeer's fantasy of making amends in a post-Ripper world:

> An I don't walk appily out no more
> Now lasses fear lad's tread,
> An mi mates call me a Bessy,
> An ah dream of all Pete's dead,
>
> An ow they come again to me,
> An we croodle out o eye
> In nests o fern an floss-seave
> An fillytails in t'sky
>
> An ah mend em all wi kindness
> As we kittle out on t'fells
> An learn us t'ease o human love
> Until there n't owt else (Morrison, 1985, 10)

It's the balladeer's new relation to the dominated streets that's noted first: the impact of the Ripper is to align him with 'Lasses'

who 'jeered at lads in porn shops' and invade public house toilets
to scrawl 'Ripper's not a psychopath/But every man in pants'.

> Everyweer in Yorkshire
> Were a creepin fear an thrill.
> At Elland Road fans chanted
> 'Ripper 12 Police Nil.' (9)

The balladeer, alienated from his mates, has passed out of a
community thrilled at the Ripper's literalization of 'men-talk'.
So in one sense it isn't true 'nowt's really altered'; the Yorkshire
weather now signifies death, not the 'stormclap' of sex (what,
imaginatively, unites the balladeer and Sutcliffe), and the balladeer's head is haunted by 'Pete's dead'. The ballad form licenses
the dialect vocabulary in which Morrison aesthetically embel-
lishes the facts of the case he's drawn from the future-novelist
Gordon Burn's '. . . *Somebody's Husband, Somebody's Son': The Story
of the Yorkshire Ripper* (1984). But while the form projects Sutcliffe
as a folkloric character, the inflexions of the balladeer's bad-faith
in his manhood introduces a perspective marked as enlightened.
It is this that makes the balladeer the true subject of the poem.
But if the ballad form looks like a way of heading off the anxiety of exploitation (the displacement of the print-story into an oral
mode creates the illusion of a found-object) it is actually the balladeer's claim of kinship with women – that which makes him
most like a reader of the *London Review of Books* – which comes
across as unwarranted or inauthentic. It is as if we cannot credit
the Yorkshire male with such a liberal ideology, and this in turn
underlines the meaning of the ballad's circularity: 'nowt's really
changed/Though Peter's out o t'way' (10).

David Peace is by contrast quite brazen in the way he seizes
on Ripper iconography to create the landscape of what has been
called Yorkshire Noir, a sub-sub-genre which makes the Ripper-
grotesque endemic: 'Everyweer in Yorkshire/Were a creepin fear
an thrill'. In *Nineteen Seventy Seven* (2000), the second of four linked
fictions, the Ripper investigation is presented as an opportunity
for officers to cover up police involvement in the abuse and murder of women. Yorkshire Noir makes literal the claim that all men
are rapists. When Peace narrates the anal rape of a prostitute (presenting it, as Barker had done, as an effect or outcome of male

frustration) it is a mark of the ubiquity, not the singularity, of male monsters: the rapist is one of the novel's protagonists and his goal is a species of kindness, to extract information about the whereabouts of his lover (missing at the height of the Ripper terror). That this lover is also a prostitute, and that she has most to fear from the Vice Squad, is one of many ways in which it is implied that the Ripper's menace is systematically reproduced throughout the institutions of law and order, and the media. DS Bob Fraser, caught in a seemingly schizophrenic relationship with the summons of his family and the siren-call of his lover (herself a pawn in a police porn-ring), is a deliberately disconcerting hero, though hero is nevertheless what the storytelling insists he is. Peace's narrative style, which is one of superficial fragmentation (developed in more substantial directions in his miners' strike novel, 1984), is well suited to Fraser's compartmentalization of domesticity, violence, suspicion and lust, which is his tactics for mastering his predicament.

> So I learnt to keep secrets, to lead two lives, to kiss my son with the same lips I kissed her with, learnt to cry alone in overlit rooms while all three of them slept, learnt to control myself, to ration, knowing there'd be famine and drought, worse plagues than this, learnt to kiss three sets of lips.
>
> (Peace, 92)

The repetition of this motif of pollution and power from Barker's novel, where it is part of the analysis of prostitution as a definition of women's labour, not their sexuality, is instructive about what is going on in both fictions. In *Blow Your House Down*, Kath mentors Brenda, who resorts to prostitution when she loses her job at the chicken processing plant and can't keep her kids, but needs help in defining the relationship with her clients economically rather than sexually: 'Always remember your mouth's your own. When he's shot his muck you've got to go back and kiss them bairns' (46–7). Peace's hero is in thrall to a fantasy that he can multiply himself, invent characters in a plot over which he will retain control (this generation of secrets is in fact the reverse of the detective's reduction of plot to causality in the unmasking of secrets). Barker's character insists on impeccable clarity in separating two lives, as if a demarcation of access to body parts can be carried over into a division between economic and affective life. As far as Angela McRobbie was concerned, Barker risked surrendering the positivism of her pornography (its grasp of the material contradictions in the lives of women who work as prostitutes) when, through the introduction of a first-person narrative of detection – Jean aping the 'Ripper' investigation – it substituted the 'atmospherics' of crime fiction, a repertoire of symbols which includes the prostitute as victim. *Blow Your House Down* converges on the genre to which *Nineteen Seventy Seven* properly belongs, but its last section is best considered as a dramatization of a struggle to return to the domestic from the realm of violence (Maggie's effort to drive out abyssal imaginings).

Barker's writing about the practical life of prostitutes is in the first instance a riposte to a regime of representation which labels prostitutes as monsters, both what Jouve has subsequently called 'Sutcliffe's text' and the codes through which it was widely interpreted. Her imitation of procedures and subject matter conventionally ascribed to pornography can likewise be understood as a strategic provocation. The theory of pornography advanced within feminism from the 1970s onwards, that pornography 'dehumanized women' (Whelehan, 156), necessarily confronts the fact that we still have a very poor understanding of 'how access to printed materials affects human behaviour' (Eisenstein, 5). This equally applies to the hypothesis that repellent imagery is aversive (as opposed to positively conditioning, in the case of the antipornography argument). This broadly behaviourist model – the territory of Anthony Burgess's novel *A Clockwork Orange* (1963), in which a teenager is cured of his 'ultraviolence' by aversive therapy – is surely inadequate to the complex of biological and cultural factors. Stanley Kubrick's film of *A Clockwork Orange* is itself a notorious example of unsupported assertions about causal links between representations and behaviours (the director categorically withdrew the film from UK distribution after claims in the House of Commons about copy-cat violence). The issues around pornography are as difficult to decide as are those concerning the power of art as a moralizing or enlightening force, though arguably more urgent. Barker's fiction is in an interesting if fraught position in these respects, tarrying with the pornographic in the service of a moral art. The same conundrum will recur in later novels in terms of the graphic representation of violence and the ideal of a poetry of protest which can be efficacious in putting a stop to war. It is perhaps not surprising that the novel strikes us as symptomatic of the contradictions in our culture, and not a transcendental analysis of those tensions. This is no more than its author would claim for it.

But in two respects *Blow Your House Down* departs strongly from the pornographic mode. One is in the motivation of the detective plot centred on Jean, and the other, in the fourth section, lies in the narration of the experience of a victim whom the attack labels as a prostitute. Jean shadows the police investigation, turning decoy into hunter in a private-enterprise 'Ripper'-hunt. The over-coded suspense in this episode contributes to Jean's disaster, her becoming a monster. She's got the wrong man, but, as the build-up of threat suggests, all men are potentially the 'Ripper'. In an sequence which echoes Paul Baumer's bayoneting of a French soldier in *All Quiet on the Western Front*, Jean stabs an ordinary punter – a family man – and death and doubt are portrayed as a double birth of this action, 'one single word, with a rush of blood like a baby splitting open a cunt, one single word: *Why?*' (132). The 'Ripper' story now becomes necessary as a means of denying the story of the family man. 'I did what he does,' Jean tells herself, revealing herself to be a version of Kelly Brown, the victim turned into the one who attacks.

Maggie is the antithesis, struggling to escape the identification that her mutilation has imprinted upon her. She works in the chicken processing plant, a scene of slaughter which picks up the baton from Upton Sinclair's revolutionary Chicago novel of the meat-packing business, *The Jungle* (1906). The bakery of *Union Street* has become a production line on which women clean up the evidence of men's killing (plucking and dressing poultry) and a heavy-duty symbol of the serial killer's clean up of the streets, elaborated in the sequence describing the slaughter of Kath. It has been argued that Barker takes a 'zoological narrative stance' to the working class in the earlier novel (Dodds); *Blow Your House Down* does something more disturbing by literalizing the ascription of animal attributes to humans in its analogy between the industrial husbandry of capitalist agribusiness and the way in which women become legitimate prey as the police and the media reproduce and condone the 'Ripper's' differentiating moral gaze. 'It was all very exciting, having a victim living in the same street. Oh, she didn't doubt the sympathy, but they were enjoying it too' (155). Maggie is Marlow to Jean's Kurtz; where Jean has gone over, for Maggie 'the abyss was at her feet' (156). In Barker's next novel, the youth worker Stephen will explicitly identify with Kurtz's 'exterminate the brutes' in Conrad's *Heart of Darkness* (1898), a kind of *reductio ad absurdum* of paternalistic social reclamation (*Liza's England*, 264). Here, however, the echo of Conrad's text (the narrator Marlow describes himself as teetering on a moral brink) has all to do with the sheer effort needed to make sense of experience and the concurrent conviction that there is no one to tell: 'It was as if her body in healing itself so quickly and so efficiently had abandoned her, had left her naked and defenceless as a seed' with something she 'could not share' (165). The closing pages of the novel acknowledge her courage with a tentative, non-verbal release from this isolation; her husband knows the feelings she believed she'd hidden. Maggie's story is the exception, a differential marked in the contrast between the image of the unwatched, roosting starlings which closes her narrative and Kath's staring face on the billboard with which Jean's narration ends.

Because Barker herself has advertised her need to move beyond the subject matter of her earliest novels, it is easy to overlook how important they are in the development of an approach to writing fiction which is based in devising formal structures of narration and thematic amplification which turn things around, eliciting our closer inspection. This is what the seven parts of *Union Street* do to a culture of feminine, working-class daily life which is reduced to a cartoon by the alternately indifferent and patronizing gaze of the dominant national culture. And in *Blow Your House Down*, the variation of narrative voice and narrative point of view revises the reader's standpoint on the legal and illegal, visible and invisible, violence on the streets of the modern city. As well as noting the way in which these narrative forms display different aspects of the novels' thematic materials, it is important to acknowledge that they are also the means of reducing the apparent authorial mediation of the story and its meanings. Barker's capacity to return to questions about violence and its representation, but in ways which her extant fiction scarcely anticipated, is dependent on her further development of these devices, particularly in the direction of dialogue, which, as we shall see, becomes explicitly more central to the form of her novels.

3

LIZA'S ENGLAND (*THE CENTURY'S DAUGHTER*) AND *THE MAN WHO WASN'T THERE*

'IT'S HISTORY': *LIZA'S ENGLAND*

In *Midnight's Children* (1981), Salman Rushdie hitched the birth of his narrator Saleem Sinai to the moment of Indian independence (perhaps in imitation of Soviet 'children of the revolution' like the novelist Alexander Solzhenitsyn, born in the wake of October 1917). There is no such political logic to Barker's character Liza Wright, née Jarrett, being front page news as 'the Century's Daughter'. The German director Edgar Reitz, in a series of films for West German television, *Heimat – Eine deutsche Chronik* (first broadcast in the UK in 1984), gave his matriarch Maria Simon the same 1900 birth date. Reitz's narrative spans the years 1919–82 so, like Barker's, it is a story of a national century from a family or personal perspective. The start of the century birth date seems freighted with symbolism, but its significance is also numerological superstition, connected strangely with public propaganda for an ideology of progress (Thomas Hardy's poem 'The Darkling Thrush', published in a national newspaper on the eve of Liza's fictional birth, was an ironic riposte to the boosterish optimism with which some greeted the new century in the last days of Victoria's reign). In this context, the author's change of title to

Liza's England makes sense. The new title signals issues of belonging and of national or perhaps 'imagined' community, rather than a mechanical parallel between an individual life path and public history. This is certainly truer to both the themes and form of the book, which is much more than its prototype in Alice Bell's retrospective on life since the Slump in *Union Street*. In that novel, the very existence of a historical perspective, invoked explicitly for the first time at the end, is sufficient to modify our apprehension of the lives of the generations succeeding Alice, and to question some of the complacent notions about progress which are a background assumption called forth by the national story.

Liza's England is a significant departure for Barker in opening out narrative time to take in both the historical past and to create a scope broad enough to accommodate historical change. Another signal development is the emergence in this novel of dialogue as the essential mode of narrative construction. *Union Street* and *Blow Your House Down* both employ a scenic method in which the relations between characters are revealed through their verbal interaction (a good example in each is an opening sequence which dramatizes the dynamics of a non-idealized family). But this technique is raised to a principle of structure and of discovery in *Liza's England*, the first of Barker's novels to employ the interview as a primary narrative device. Stephen is a social worker charged with persuading Liza to accept rehousing, the first of a line of protagonists whose engagement with an outsider figure is framed by the regimes of professional care. In *Regeneration* the device of the interview is supplied by therapeutic encounters. In that novel, W.H.R. Rivers is himself presented as learning the nuances of the psychoanalytic session from his earlier anthropological investigations, interrogating Pacific islanders to discover kinship patterns. In *Border Crossing* the device reappears in the repetition of meetings between a forensic psychologist and a defendant, and in *Another World* in the form of taped oral history interviews.

The significance of the interview as a means of provoking a plurality of narrative points of view should be evident. Most characteristically in Barker's writing it is a counterweight to the verbal and conceptual intelligence, and the pattern making, of the third-person narrator, a means of granting a degree of independence to the characters' world views. This is the most important of the Dostoyevskyan elements in Barker's work. In

Crime and Punishment (1866), for instance, Dostoyevsky narrated the story of Raskolnikov, the student-murderer, and prospective Christian convert, through dialogues in which the major characters are counterpointed with each other. The reader approaches an understanding of Raskolnikov and his situation by trying to reconcile the angles of vision acquired in these juxtapositions. The Russian literary critic Mikhail Bakhtin (1895–1975), influential in the West as a theorist of the social dimensions of language and semiotics, described Dostoyevsky's narrative technique as both dialogic and polyphonic – having the qualities of social speech and of a musical composition which counterpoints a number of voices – in his book *Problems of Dostoyevsky's Poetics* (1929). The political and ideological significance of such techniques lay in the freeing of character from the authority of the narrator; the novel became a utopian space in which contesting points of view are not subordinated to an overmastering order of meaning. This is similar to an argument Salman Rushdie would make in the wake of the publication of *The Satanic Verses*, and to literary criticism by the fatwah of the Ayatollah Khomeini: 'Literature is the one place in any society where, within the secrecy of our own heads, we can hear *voices talking about everything in every possible way*' (Rushdie, 429). Barker is a master of these techniques, and among the most interesting thing she does with them is holding open the process by which contending meanings (some of them rooted in gender and class divisions, some in historical change) are unified or sometimes homogenized by familiar narrative forms and by familiar forms of historical consciousness.

We can gauge the distance Barker has come if we think of Stephen as a new use of the position Kelly occupies in the structure of *Union Street* (as Liza is a revision of Alice Bell). The girl's encounters with Alice are primarily symbolic and formal (a repetition of the same incident from different points of view). Georg Lukacs, the influential Hungarian Marxist theorist of the novel, in an essay titled 'Narrate or Describe?' (1936), lingered over the fact that Tolstoy narrates the horse race in *Anna Karenina* (1873–77) *twice*: this example leads to Lukacs's distinction between novelists who employ narration from the standpoint of a participant, and those (he has in mind Zola and Flaubert) who describe 'from the standpoint of an observer' (Lukacs, 111). Barker's working-class novels have been criticized for their affinity with nineteenth-century naturalism (which means above all the novelist strategies of Zola), that is for the way the observing narrator fixes the characters in terms of 'physical and manual' detail, from the point of view of an objectifying observer: thus *Union Street* has been described as '*about* the working class, not of it' (Dodd and Dodd, 122–4). But this reading underestimates the extent to which Barker was already endeavouring to make us experience events, rather than have us mere spectators, and this concern is a key motivation of her developing narratorial style. Dialogue will become Barker's primary device for narrating from the standpoint of participants, a narration necessarily conflicted by contrasting points of view, but also one which accepts that the condition of dialogue does not lend itself to closure.

In *Liza's England*, the encounter in dialogue between Liza and Stephen is reiterated through a developing relationship. This relationship changes Stephen, who in one sense represents the 'objective' ideological regime which produces housing policy. Furthermore, while motivating and naturalizing the recollection of a century's worth of social history, the device of the interview opens up a sequence of surprising parallels between contemporary Britain and Liza's England of the Great War, the Slump, the Second World War and post-war affluence. This is interesting not least for its commentary on the callow appeals to historical continuity made during the period of Thatcher's premiership, notably in relation to the Falklands war and unemployment. Liza's unemployed and emasculated husband Frank abandons the family to go on the tramp, resurfacing in the workhouse, months later, for Liza to lay out. This is a pointed rejoinder to the Tory Secretary of State Norman Tebbit, whose story of his out-of-work father encapsulated the shift from the Keynesian goal of full-employment to the 1980s ideology of therapeutic economic pain: 'He didn't riot. He got on his bike and looked for work, and he kept looking until he found it' (*Times*, 16 October 1981, 1).

In *Liza's England*, Barker is working with some of the fictional strategies and the materials for which she has been most celebrated, as a postmodern historical novelist of war and violence. For instance, the opening provides us with the idea of 'time-travel' as a way of thinking about memory, narrative and historical consciousness, as well as the novel's own procedures for connecting the temporally distinct. The phrase introduces Stephen's relationship to his parents, a relationship of which he is a spectator in his role as a professional who has been educated out of his class: 'those three hours on the train came to seem more and more like time-travel, a slipping back through railway cuttings and tunnels not merely into his own past, but into the country's past' (35). Liza is a less self-conscious time-traveller, going back with the aid of the family souvenirs stored in her tin chest, and her familiarity with 'all the stories about them' (23).

The sense of precariousness which in Barker's first two novels haunts the built environment of terraced housing and factory, as well as the cultural and economic viability of working-class communities, is brought to a crisis in Liza's virtual isolation as a survivor amidst demolition. Where Alice Bell is assigned to a Home as she was too infirm to stay in her own home, Liza must be rehoused to permit slum clearance: a kind of apocalypse has come to the North East (we are still in the geographical neighbourhood of *Union Street*, as reference to familiar street names confirms). This crisis is incarnate in the Clagg Lane estate, a public housing project which is represented, in contrast to Union Street, by a predominantly male group of juveniles, and in particular by their subversion of the youth club notionally supervised by Stephen and other social workers. The aggression of these kids is superficial, for the class which has come to be defined by its council housing is on the defensive (Hanley). The place itself is a maze, its road signs 'uprooted or turned back to front, as if the inhabitants of Clagg Lane expected an invasion' (11). The humour here turns on nostalgia for the legendary social unity of the Second World War (when road signs were removed to foil German parachutists), and provides the first in a series of parallels between military and civil life which challenge us to reckon just how civil ordinary life really is, and to rethink some of our images of historical England. In this Barker's treatment of urban ruin anticipates Derek Jarman's film *The Last of England* (1987), whose images of the militarization of civil space were shot at Beckton gas works in East London, where Stanley Kubrick had the year previously staged the Vietnam battle scenes of his *Full Metal Jacket* (Wymer, 112).

Compared to the earlier novels, *Liza's England* is a more ambitious treatment of the intersection of the worlds of men and women, worlds which have been continually constructed and reconstructed by ideology, experience and analysis. As a narrative grounded in the social history of working-class women it adds a chronological dimension to the unflinching representation of the degradations of ordinary life. But with its simultaneous interest in the figure of the male at odds with formerly dominant masculine codes (Stephen is in this respect a much developed version of Richard Scaife) it begins to open up what the focus on women had previously occluded, that is a phenomenology of the patriarchal role, what it is to live with the expectation that you are a man and must act as one. One could say that *Liza's England* attempts a more panoramic account of living in a gendered world, a world in which your gender is as much a determinant of your flourishing as your environment.

The present of the novel reveals two realms of masculinity, one associated with the apparently lawless youth of the estate, the other with the professions to which Stephen's education has assigned him. The division between them appears almost total, but so too does the separation between Stephen and his father. It is symptomatic of the change of direction in Barker's writing that the scene in which Stephen's relations with his father are brought to crisis is a rewriting involving a kind of gender reassignment: in *Union Street* the haemorrhaging, prematurely dying blue-collar worker is nursed by his wife; here he is nursed by his son, casting the latter into a traditionally feminine role (significantly, the only representational norm for the male as nurse is the ambivalent image of the soldier cradling the wounded comrade, inaugurated in literature by Walt Whitman's American Civil War poem 'The Wound Dresser'). Shifting the caring role to the male, Barker sets up a number of resonant analogies. Some of these are captured in the image with which the two generations are separated. The Leeds-born poet Tony Harrison entitled a sonnet describing the education which divided him from his working-class father 'Book Ends': 'what's still between 's/not the thirty or so years, but books, books, books' (Harrison, 126). Barker's father and son are not facing away from each other, but non-connectors, 'like a pair of electric plugs that wouldn't fit into each other' (40). Given the male monopoly over mechanical and electrical trades it is not surprising that all manner of connectors which 'mate', from pipes to plugs, are gendered male and female; the image of gender's internal divisions is tacitly earthed, by Barker, in the everyday representation of gender as binary.

Divisions between men that arise from work are the most public, and hence among the most damaging. Stephen cannot help himself assuming that to a veteran of the factory floor his own job making decisions about child protection just does not qualify as work. What is really unnatural to the father, however, is the absence of necessity, his son's freedom to swap that career for another one, this time finding 'ways of passing the time' for unemployed youngsters (38). This relationship of professionalized care has already been criticized by Brian, the one boy on the estate Stephen can identify with, because his stance – 'sceptical, intelligent, bitter' – echoes his own educational advantage and alienation. Brian is bitter enough to observe that helping the unemployed is 'the only growth industry there is' (13–14). A kind of prototype of Billy Prior, a character who bridges the realms of intellectual freedom and material necessity, his personal reserve gives way under the pressure of Stephen's sympathy to reveal a background of paternal domestic violence.

But it is nursing his terminally ill father that tests Stephen's identity most strenuously. Unwelcome confessions of his father's sexuality are as much a mutual obstacle as the father's silence about Stephen's homosexuality; that these broken exchanges take place in bed, the son a surrogate for the wife, multiplies the irony of terminal intimacies. The helplessness of the bystander to death undermines Stephen's sense of managerial competence, his self-image as a member of the officer caste. In these scenes Barker is beginning to explore the relationship between experience and expression, world and representation, which will become the hallmark of her fiction. *Liza's England* approaches these themes through symbol and metaphor; its characters are not fully privileged to analyze, in terms of some professional discourse, the way their own lives are held between what they do and what they say about it. The 'clot of blood, like a lump of black liver' which Stephen takes from his father's mouth becomes an emblem in the relay of shock, standing for the father's repressions and then for Stephen's melancholia (120). His emotional reticence, the familiar pressure in the throat, is turned into a figure for masculinity itself: 'as if his father's silence had somehow got in and impacted there' (123). Stephen is a sceptic about symptoms, and anxious about the way his sore throat might be read as a kind of Freudian truism, 'the link with his father's death was too obvious' (191). But dealing with death – Stephen masturbates out of anger at its claim on him – is a lost art. It is however what connects Stephen's and Liza's experience, what they recognize in each other as anger over premature loss, and what connects war and peace.

Liza is portrayed as a victim not of male power but of male vulnerability. In another re-gendering of material from *Union Street*, Liza Goddard's memory of smashed bird's eggs is now rhymed not with the daughter's ova, but with the son's testes 'looking like tiny crushable eggs'. Cradling her child's scrotum Liza Wright held 'the potential power of a man's body, and its weakness'. This pairing of might and vulnerability is nowhere more evident than in war, which for Liza is the abiding fact about boys: '[t]hey could take him away and kill him' (82). As her brother Edward was killed in the First World War, so her son Tommy will be killed in the Second.

It is hard to read Barker's treatment of war in *Liza's England* without looking for anticipations of some of the themes of *Regeneration*. But even as we do this, we are in a position to note how different are the formal means with which this material is articulated into a social vision. The trilogy's revisionist levelling of the hierarchy of front line and home front experience is certainly foreshadowed in the way *Liza's England* parallels the experience of men and women during the Great War. The workers in the munitions factory are 'canary girls' because of the yellow tinge to their skin (the effect of pitric acid) but additionally, like mine canaries, they are exposed to a dangerous atmosphere that requires the use of respirators like those worn in the trenches (Billy Prior is nicknamed the battalion 'Canary', his asthma making him sensitive to phosphene gas). The respiratory casualties of modern mine and factory labour outnumber those English soldiers gassed in France, but no one wrote their 'Dulce et decorum est'.

Liza's England explores the theme of the wound and of wounds to the psyche (in the academic humanities the word trauma now refers primarily to the latter). Trauma is at the heart of *Regeneration* and its sequels, but viewed through the lens of a revised Freudian framework of ideas brought into play through the fictionalization of the work of W.H.R. Rivers. *Regeneration* is a novel much concerned with rational and scientific understanding of human suffering. *Liza's England* is more visceral, more immediate (despite its framework of a memorial reconstruction of the past). Its challenge to the reader to reconfigure major themes of English social history – war, production and consumption, the family, education, the role of the state, progress and decline – is bound up with the emotional force with which Liza's perspective is communicated.

Wounding and death in combat – the horror of modern war – are not represented directly, anymore than they are in *Regeneration*, but indirectly, through analogy, through prolepsis (a rhetorical foreshadowing) and through the coping strategies of those who survive to experience bereavement. We have seen how the hazards of Liza's war work echo the ordnance of the Western Front (gas, high explosive). Barker also reveals an interest in the prose techniques of Siegfried Sassoon by the way she shapes the idyll of friendship interrupted by the declaration of war: river-bank mud ironically anticipates the landscape of Flanders, just as Sassoon had used the huntsman's fear of barbed-wire to undercut naïve bellicose enthusiasms (48). But it is the legacy of war which most concerns Barker in this novel, the story of the survivor and the bereaved.

The survivor is Frank Wright, a war invalid who returns as a spiritualist, 'resurrecting an entire neighbourhood' (a locally raised Pals battalion). The episode is testimony to Barker's visual imagination, echoing Stanley Spencer's iconography of the resurrection of soldiers and civilians in famous post-war murals (the memorial chapel at Burghclere) and canvases (Hyman and Wright, 44–7, 120–3). Voices pour from Frank's wounded throat, and the narrative provides us with as many orientations to this mode of public mourning. Frank's own sense of vocation is code for symptoms of trauma, of extreme experience which has not been integrated. His vocalizations are related to hallucinations of dead comrades (84). To Liza the performance is an affront to the bereaved, a pretence, an impersonation of the absent, a mere parroting of familiar accents and biographies (62). This illusion takes on, however, a metaphorical colouring – 'Mouths, silent, mud-stopped, gaped open and spoke. Lungs, gas-blistered, blood-frothed, drew in air again' – which suggests continuities with the language of the war poets, a vehicle, ultimately, of a national 'memory' (61).

The social historian Jay Winter has argued that '[h]owever "modern" the Great War was, its immediate repercussion was to deepen and not transform older languages of loss and consolation' (Winter, 76). Spiritualism, 'the private denial of death' in the words of the historian David Cannadine, is a prime example of a reversion to Victorian sentiments (Winter, 57). This is not least because spiritualism involves a 'slide from metaphors of remembering those who have died to the metaphysics of life after death' (Winter, 76). But spiritualism was also a mode of resistance to official cultures of remembrance, a factor which is of particular importance given the decision not to repatriate the remains of servicemen to Britain. Tours to the battlefields would become a significant dimension of post-war remembrance only for those who could afford to travel; before the erection of urban and village war memorials in the 1920s, the consolation of spiritualist contact with the dead filled a vacuum in traditional practices of mourning.

Barker will return to spiritualism in *The Man Who Wasn't There* and in the trilogy, as an explicit counterpart to the medicalization of memory in discourses about mourning and trauma. Frank's parroting may be a mere rote repetition from Liza's point of view (an unwelcome restoration of the missing); from a Freudian perspective it is symptomatic of the compulsion to repeat past events in the present, a repetition revealed in his nightmares. The tensions between spiritualism as denial and the ambitions of therapeutic practice to work through traumatic repetition to integration (a remembering to forget) are represented in the novel in the analogies between Frank and Stephen as survivors. References to the throat have a double significance, as symptom and symbol, pointing towards the paired ideas of repression and expression, the destination of experience in pathology and art respectively.

Frank's vocation is implicitly compared to that of the most famous war poet, Wilfred Owen, who justified his return to France to his mother as an aspiration to give voice to the fallen, and to intercede for them: 'I came out in order to help these boys . . . by watching their sufferings that I may speak of them as a pleader can' (Owen, 351). The reciprocal relationship with the canonical writing of the Great War which defines Barker's fictional recreations of the period is already evident here. Among the war stories told Liza by the mutilated Ben is one that recalls the anecdote of the charge of the headless lance-corporal in Remarque's *All*

Quiet on the Western Front (1929). This has been used to impugn the authority of Remarque's hugely influential novel (which has been burdened with expectations of documentary faithfulness), but in Barker's hands it becomes the vehicle for another image of the male as carer, and hence a way of complicating the repertoire of national war stories (Eksteins, 282).

Liza's own century is a story of loss, first Edward, then Tom, who is no sooner incarnated in a newsreel than he is announced dead. Yet military exploits remain a potent distraction from hard times. Brian claims that 'it needs a war' to sort out the dereliction of the contemporary working-class: 'Look at the Falklands . . . . It was the only *real* thing that'd ever happened to them'. The invocation of official history – 'That's how they did it last time, isn't it' – is evidence of the power of militarist ideology, even over a character who is usually immune to the state's propaganda: 'People know what they are doing in a war. They know they are alive' (196).

The armature on which all the foregoing themes and dramas are constructed is Liza's life, her more-than-survival of her mother's neglect and hatred to become the single-mother to two genera-tions, and to witness the beginning of the revolution in women's education. Kath's prospects come to equal, on a private level, a century's sacrifice, the lives of brother, husband and son, as well as Liza's labours. This is the substance of the rewriting in *Liza's England* of the account of abortion in *Union Street*. Liza's refusal of the danger and the respite of abortion (her daughter Eileen is pregnant) stands rather portentously for woman's dedication to the life which the State so callously wastes. But Liza's decision is also a reassertion of a selfhood which at this crisis has come, in an unfamiliar image, to be something almost dispensable, 'a skin to be sloughed off' (206). This metaphor will resurface in *Double Vision* as a symptomatic self-description of the childhood murderer Peter Wingrave, a character who persists through mimicry of others. The fact that Liza will die at the hands of children shouldn't sanc-tify her; she has sacrificed but is not a sacrificial victim. Her story is not in opposition to her attackers' but transects it. The voices that tell her to kill Kath are she asserts 'her experience', part of her and not an aberration, illness or deviance to be 'tamed by pills' or 'traivialized by condescension' (242).

In a literal sense Liza's tale is a kind of survivor's song, the elegiac account of the one whom battle spares. She comes to replicate Frank's spiritualist ventriloquism, the ghost road of his particular gift of tongues: to Stephen, her stories have the effect of repopulating the derelict streets which progress has cleared (169). As the novel's last witness (a role to be reprised by Geordie in *Another World*) she stands for both coming through the horrors of existence, but also against a kind of forgetfulness on the part of those who succeed her. In *Liza's England* this amnesia is produced by money. Rehearsing arguments about the break-up of working-class community by a culture of consumption (notably voiced in Richard Hoggart's *The Uses of Literacy* of 1957), Liza insists that the meaning of her century is loss, not the daily losses which systemic inequity inflicts, but loss of 'a way of life, a way of treating people' (218). But Liza turns out to have more faith in the future than Stephen, who presides professionally over the cancellation of the future for the area's working-class youth (he is, to use Orwell' *Nineteen Eighty-Four* as an analogy, Winston Smith to her prole-wife). The novel is most eloquent about this much-advertised contradiction between affluence and community at the level of its imagery. Liza is fascinated by a television show contestant struggling to remember, and thus win, items she'd watched 'passing by her on a conveyor belt', and is moreover drawn into sympathetic identification with the way the stuff that 'stuck in your mind' was not the stuff you wanted to. The show, which was called *The Generation Game* (1971–82), becomes a symbol for the division between the past, which is slipping away, and a future plenitude of commodities which is, in a different way, out of reach. This is rendered more complex by the echo of the mechanism responsible for the fugitive promise of the scratting heaps, those 'tiny nuggets' of coal brought by conveyor; 'the buckets coming in along the wires . . . opening to release what looked even at this distance like a shower of black rain' (158). The practical community of the coal 'gleaners' is juxtaposed with the wholly mediated community of viewers, and their weak aspiration to be in a position to help themselves to TV's prize cornucopia. Yet the show elicits, as exampled in Liza's reaction, both a fellow-feeling and a resonant symbol of the incalculable in remembering and forgetting.

Economics is the engine of history as both change and oblivion: 'It's history, this pub,' a tangible trace of the past and about to be consigned to the past (248). *Liza's England* has this double perspective, which risks compromising its exacting retrieval and representation of prior beliefs and social arrangements with a hallowing of the past because it has gone. This risk is incarnated in the person of Liza, who seems to contradict the catastrophic character of her own experience with her regret for its passing: after all the boys of the estate may need a war, but they don't have to go to one. But the novel makes a virtue of the differences between living and remembering, and it does so through the triangulation with Stephen's callowness, his primarily theoretical apprehension of the passing of an environment. *Liza's England* is eloquent about the lives broken by England's industrial ghettoes, but also about the values which were forged there. Its juxtaposition of the ratios of Liza past and present, and of Liza and Stephen, help ensure it steers clear of both despair and nostalgia. Barker has stated that 'people are geared to surviving in a particular environment' (Garland, 195). She was talking about myths of rehabilitation, but the remark is illuminating too about Barker's fictions of urban poverty and violence. This biological model of learning implies a political stance (the bleak determinism which Stephen opts for after his exposure to the estate) but it is also a historical conception of the individual's values as shaped by the limits and incentives of a material way of life. 'Not the good old days' because 'sixty years' hard labour' (261, 278). But the ending of it – the extinction of the community apotheosized in the brutal and pointless attack on Liza – rebuts the condescension of progress. The end of Liza, and the end of the history of the locale are also the end of the dialogue with Stephen. As we have just seen, this concurrence of endings falls short of the promise of either conceptual or affective closure, an issue which will recur in later fictions, notably *Regeneration*. The power of dialogue to keep rival conceptions in play has its price in the difficulty of bringing that process to an end.

THE MAN WHO WASN'T THERE: 'THE SHADOW SEEMED MORE SOLID THAN THE PLANE'

Barker's fourth novel, *The Man Who Wasn't There* (1989), appears initially to return us to the territory of *Blow Your House Down* and the struggles of the deserted mother, the mother who must negotiate the opportunities of the sex industry and the demands of a fractured domesticity. But *The Man Who Wasn't There* is a comedy.

It is also centred on the point of view of a child. And although the scene initially appears near-contemporary, the novel is historical, in fact doubly so. The never-replaced railings of this seaside town, an unofficial memorial to wartime salvage campaigns, are an external index of post-war austerity Britain. But Colin's re-enactments – we meet him 'one eye open for snipers' in his fantasy role as 'Gaston' of the French Resistance – are the novel's primary symbol for a historical moment which is after, but not over, the war.

Reading back from *Regeneration*, it is perhaps more obvious where Barker is headed with *The Man Who Wasn't There*. The novel is an un-dogmatic and nuanced commentary on the 'popular masculine pleasure-culture of war' (Dawson, 4), the 'national image ... [as] an aggressively militant warrior nation' (Paris, 11) and their intersection with the iconography of the war against Nazism. This topic would receive extensive coverage by historians and cultural critics at the end of the century, an analytic engagement which was typically introduced through recollections of the (male) authors' own war play or consumption of war culture (Gilroy, Connelly and Dawson). Here is more evidence of the way Barker's fiction interacts with and anticipates, rather than simply responds to, the developing historiography of Britain at war.

But to readers of Barker's earlier Virago novels, the exploration of adolescent investments in the 'warrior nation' in this short fiction would have seemed less necessary than whimsical, obvious reference point being the BBC drama of the wartime French Resistance, *Secret Army* (1977–79), and the parodying of the earlier show in the popular situation comedy '*Allo 'Allo* (1982–92). Barker has claimed that 'the dominance of '*Allo 'Allo*, which has almost made the serious treatment of the French Resistance impossible, is actually an asset to the book' (Monteith et al., 2005, 120). If this means that there was a kind of popular–cultural licence to overlook the terrors and controversies of the occupation, then this commentary seems to underplay the way the novel elicits serious reflections from its handling of child's play. The amusing collage of motifs drawn from post-war cinematic glosses on the war (less recognizable now as this iconography is supplanted by Spielberg's Second World War) is also an evaluation on many levels of the repression of history in the reproduction of cultural norms.

Barker's interest in the problem of masculine socialization reveals, in fact, a certain logic, in parallel with trends in academic and historiographical discourse. The absent and menacing male of the early novels (a determinant of women's struggle to construct the practical family within the normative framework erected by the social matrix) is, in this novel, a significance-laden gap – 'Vacancies', 'Blank' – which tropes the child's passage into masculinity (10, 157). This absence points to the symbolic work required to produce the phallic warrior male who is a foundation of the social order. The progression towards this problem can be traced through the rewriting of masculine impotence in *Union Street* (the organically ruined factory worker John Scaife) as Stephen's nursing of his father in *Liza's England*. Liza may not have imposed herself on her century, but she has come through, not as a deluded parrot-keeper, like Felicité in Flaubert's *Un Coeur Simple* (1877), but simply used up. Stephen has it all to do, his work of producing society framed by a welfare institution, his work of coming into adulthood shadowed by differences from his father. At 12, Colin is a counterpart of Kelly Brown, another fatherless child who seeks surrogates for an absent father but who is far more harshly treated by the grown-up world this longing draws her towards. The comic form sees Colin cocooned in a developmental matrix characterized by Oedipal sexual fantasy and libidinal investments in violence, rather than exposed to the law of the street.

A pariah in his grammar school, Colin's status as misfit is most exactingly delineated in the interaction between his mother's shame and his own, each correlated with socially induced guilt about non-normative family structures. Viv has been knocked up, made pregnant, during the war: 'people grabbed what they could' (157). For her the war will not be over for a long time, because its widely romanticized furlough from peace-time sexual mores – the erotic opportunity of the emergency – has left her with the 20-year task of raising a son. It is as if the unfinished business of 1945 stretched out beyond the Cuban Missile Crisis of 1962 – as in fact it did. Colin is her Cold War, the legacy of the heat of wartime extra-marital romance.

Colin fills his life imaginatively with fantasies of war to try to match the souvenirs his classmates possess in the more palpable form of their veteran dads. *Daddy, what did YOU do in the Great*

War (the text of a poster admonishing pre-conscription non-volunteers to take up arms) is mobilized now not as a reproof to men who stayed at home but as an affirmation of the legitimate masculinization of the offspring of veterans. Colin makes up war experience just as his mates do; but for him the activity is over-determined as exploratory sexual play and resistance to authority. His Resistance-script, a melodrama of French underground intelligence, Nazi occupation, of risk and betrayal, is presented in the novel by typographical differentials, in italics and in the conventional format of the printed stage play. As well as being make-believe about resistance to the Occupation, it is also fantasy resistance to the enemy forces which perturb Colin's existence. The most notable of these are his pubescent sexuality and the masculine and class codes of the local Grammar School, to which the bright working-class boy has been recruited by the 11-plus examination. Functioning like the Officers Training Corps (OTC), the school expects Colin to join an educational officer-class and leave behind the friends he has made among the 'Other Ranks' of the Secondary Modern, the true scene of resistance to middle-class values (Willis).

There is a dream-like quality to Colin's waking reveries in a strictly Freudian sense: his day-dreams are marked by the presence of a daily residue, matter derived from the practical challenges of the novel's 60-hour time-span. And the novel transforms some of these elements into symbols with meanings not manifest to the boy. The Resistance-script is an ironic inflation of Colin's ordinary, but from an egocentric perspective, crisis-ridden life. Like his counterparts in the Resistance, he must become a forger of documents, but bathetically, when his mum won't sign his school report. His work as courier is running an errand (and, humiliatingly, being short-changed). The name of his alter-ego, *Gaston*, is taken from a list on a Grammar School blackboard covered in a language he cannot understand. Pretending to be in the war also gets mixed up with his sexual curiosity and his anxieties about his mother's sexuality.

Colin's war story is a supplement to his mother's, which is designed to account for the blank on his birth certificate, the absence of the father: 'He didn't bugger off, Colin. He was shot down' (14). The Resistance-script is thus Colin's part in the family's work to 'forge the bugger' (11), to create the fiction of normal family life (having parents concerned enough to sign your report).

> It was a moving story, the way Viv told it. Colin was moved. He was moved again a few nights later when he saw the same story on the screen of the Gaumont. A plane exploded, violins swelled, tears glistened, a young girl walked home alone.
> He'd never believed anything Viv said since. (32)

While he can't believe her, the social pressures to have a war story are nevertheless irresistible. The leaders of the break-time war games are the boys 'whose fathers had been in the war' (32–3). Colin's is a sceptical and contradictory elaboration of his mother's cinematic falsehood because it refracts his pubescent anxieties about becoming a man.

The most striking thing about the development of Colin's resistance-play over the 3 days of the narrative is not its own narrative pace (there are plenty of deaths), but the pace at which Colin's identifications are revised. 'Gaston', the British boy with perfect French, is ultimately supplanted in the story by the effeminate cross-dressing 'Bernard'. The plot detours through 'Gaston's' doing away with 'Vivienne' as a punishment for her fraternization with the enemy, before 'Gaston' the double-agent is fed to his Nazi employers, an apposite emblem of the kind of fantasy war in which the victor has no blood on his hands. The End follows Bernard's decision to take his chances in France, rather than evacuate by R. A. F. Lysander (the plane Colin has modelled and hung from his bedroom ceiling); this imagined scene bookends the movie scene Viv appropriated to explain his father's absence, and thus offers one kind of resolution to the anxieties of growing up without a man about the house (the aetiology of Bernard's penchant for women's clothing in the resistance play).

The novel, like *Liza's England*, does not presume that the only presences are flesh-and-blood humans and fictional characters: *The Man Who Wasn't There* has its roll call of ghosts and apparitions, from the features beneath the skin that seem to be bursting through Colin's boyish face (92) to the revenant of a missing airman encountered by Mrs Stroud. The apparition that bears the most weight is the Man in Black, who emerges, literally, from the resistance play (thus representing a different order of threat to The Man in 'Kelly Brown'), and who confronts the feverish Colin in his mother's bedroom. The gothic elements in this scene are put in their place via Colin's resolve 'to stand where he stood', which leaves the identity of the figure nicely undecided between the missing father and Colin's future (153).

That future, it is implied, is a matter of growing out of false-hoods, as with Mrs Stroud's admission that her spiritualist 'gift' was adapted to telling people 'what they *want* to be told' (120). When he finally rejects his mother's theatre of remembrance – 'She doesn't bloody well *know!*' – he can bring his own resis-tance play to an end (157). Colin is simultaneously growing out of the public culture of remembering and forgetting which was disseminated through Britain's cinemas in the 1950s, an era of large audiences for domestically produced features among which war films were consistently high earners: *Odette*; *The Wooden Horse* (1950); *The Cruel Sea* (1952); *The Dam Busters* (1955); *Reach for the Sky* (1956); *Ill Met by Moonlight* (1957) (Ramsden, 62–3).

> he tried to look at the pictures in his film annuals, but all the films were jumbled together in his head. He was tired of them anyway: the clipped, courageous voices, the thoroughly decent chaps, the British bombs that always landed on target, the British bombers that always managed to limp home. They told lies, he thought. They said it was easy to be brave. (151)

This is as near the novel gets to crediting Colin with an inkling into the misrepresentations that the national culture seems unable to grow out of, in particular sanitized, meaningful narratives of past military action and contradictory ideals of the warrior male, even as styles and media are transformed by an economy of novelty.

The same device which makes possible the comic elaboration of the crises of adolescence is also a fruitful perspective on the way history gets made in the service of the present. That Colin's appro-priation of the representational repertoire of his war-shadowed era is opportunistic goes without saying; his fantasies would only appear pathological if they became ossified, a permanent reflex for interpreting his social world and his internalization of its chal-lenges. But the war cinema of the 1950s is an element in a national culture which, as it 'promotes the martial spirit, elevates the warrior to heroic status and romanticizes war', has preserved the identity of 'warrior nation' through a century of change (Paris, 11).

It has been suggested that 'the film Colin watches is probably Ronald Neame's *The Man Who Never Was* (1956)' (Monteith et al., 117), but, title apart, there is no clear connection between this movie of strategic deception set in England (screenplay by Nigel Balchin, author of two great wartime novels, *Darkness Falls from the Air* and *The Small Back Room*), and either what Colin views, or what he fantasizes. Indeed, it could be argued that the scene in question, dwelling on the motifs of fear before a parachute jump and the 'roman candle' (slang for the failure of a 'chute to deploy), alludes to fictional narratives centred on bogus representations of military escapades: Evelyn Waugh's *Sword of Honour* trilogy (1952–61), and in particular Ludovic's retreat from Crete, and even more strikingly, Graham Swift's *Shuttlecock* (1981), in which a son comes to doubt the veracity of his father's published memoir of parachuting into occupied France. But these identifications are beside the point, for Barker's citations of an extant corpus of war representations in this novel seem to be deliberately fuzzy. In contrast to her next work, where the fiction is explicitly connected to a body of existing literature and art through quotation, allusion, references and acknowledgements, *The Man Who Wasn't There* presents its cinematic source material from a consumer's view point. What matters is that two inveterate cinema-goers have seen the same scenes. Viv is so habituated to movie-palace escapism that she buys a ticket on the night of her father's funeral. And Colin's one act of genuine undercover work is evading the film classification by slipping in through the fire doors.

With her third and fourth novels, Barker's material was consciously shifted from the near-contemporary to the historical, and from the world of women to the world of men and women. Her next phase, which would establish her status, and define her mode as a novelist, would amplify both the practice of historical reconstruction and the degree of representational self-consciousness in her writing. It would additionally attempt a further revision of the treatment of gender, positing that the Great War was not exclusively *male* experience. *Regeneration* and its sequels would further develop the formal discoveries of *Liza's England*, centred on the therapeutic dialogue, and find new ways of exploiting the potency

of rendering the past through citing the repertoire of its representations, a method which is brilliantly elaborated for comic
purposes in *The Man Who Wasn't There*. But these are not merely
transitional works, no matter how uncharacteristic of the later
phases of Barker's novel writing. Each represents a coherent and
fully expressive working out of complex problems of construction, and complex values, within a distinctive fictional world.

4

REGENERATION, THE EYE IN THE DOOR AND THE GHOST ROAD

> Only a military hospital can really show you what war is.
> (Remarque, 186)

The hospitals described by German novelist Erich Maria Remarque in his internationally best-selling *All Quiet on the Western Front* of 1929 are literally a stage on which to produce the spectacle of war's material destructiveness: 'the damaged limb had been hoisted up into the air on a kind of gallows: underneath the wound itself there is a dish for the pus to drip into' (Remarque, 185). But the theatre of atrocity is played out only before those who are party to the killing; families know nothing of what has become of their sons. Remarque's soldiers are mute bodies, reduced to their digestive systems and drilled as killing machines. They adapt to war by disowning their humanity; pressing themselves into the earth for cover, it is as if they were reversing evolution.

Barker affirms that a military hospital alone 'can really show you what war is' with her treatment of Craiglockhart, an Army facility in Edinburgh whose function is restoring officers to mental health and returning them to battle. Out of sight of the public, in its wards and consulting rooms, the terrors of war manifest themselves, and coping strategies are learned, but in the form of psychic conflicts, psychosomatic injury and therapeutic demonstrations. The contrast between Remarque and Barker can be read as witness to changing conceptions of the damage war inflicts on people. This is particularly significant in relation to our own era, when Post-Traumatic Stress Disorder represents a literal return of the repressed. The West has, since the 1960s, developed a style of warfare which has progressively hidden the human costs of war by replacing manpower with firepower, a style of war predicated on minimal friendly casualties (Lewis). In the same period, starting with Vietnam, Western societies have belatedly acknowledged that war damages minds as well as bodies.

But if the use of Craiglockhart as setting for a novel of war points to a contemporary preoccupation with psychological rather than physical trauma, and with individual memory, it also points to another form of memory, the public sense of the past incarnated in culture (stories, myths, popular history and literature). Craiglockhart had a crucial role in the stories of Britain's most famous First World War poets; it, rather than the Western Front, can be considered the site of origin of modern war literature (Wilfred Owen was encouraged to write about his nightmares by Craiglockhart's ergotherapist, A. J. Brock) (Rawlinson, 120). Barker's sequence of novels has a productive, intricate and controversial relationship with this anti-heroic literature of disillusionment and protest. It both appropriates and seems to go beyond it. Exploring the relationship between the inarticulable and the ways in which war can be made culturally meaningful, between the wound and its symptoms, Barker's fiction is at once a historical reconstruction and a reckoning with the legacy of war.

Regeneration and its sequels have a multi-layered relation to the Great War and its subsequent mediations. Barker has talked about sticking 'to historical facts' (Stephenson, 176), but has also explained that she sought to avoid revisiting familiar ground: 'I didn't see the point of writing an anti-war novel that only examined the tragedy that is already part of the fabric of our national consciousness' (Monteith, 2004, 27). One way she saw herself promoting new apprehensions of the Great War was in having brought out 'a subtext in what people believed they were hearing' when they listened to the voices of 1914–18 (Nixon, 18). So the novel is about the past but also about the ways we apprehend the past, what Barker has called 'the ethics of historical memory in the present', a subject addressed directly in the novel *Another World* of 1998 (Brannigan, 'Interview', 2005, 369).

The most salient dimension of the Great War as it is known to the majority of Barker's readers is the literature of the war, notably the 'protest poetry' of Siegfried Sassoon and Wilfred Owen. In the last decades of the twentieth century, this small, unrepresentative corpus of writing became central to encounters with both history and poetry in British schools. Turning these cultural heroes into fictional protagonists involves substantial risks, as well as presenting opportunities for fictional engagements with the historical. Barker's own status as an examinable author on the A Level syllabus (and the repute and the sales that accompany this) was bound up with how her trilogy invited broader reflection on the ways in which later generations have represented the Great War. The device of Prior palpably raises the question of what is at stake in creating dissonant, retrospective images of the conflict, such as Theatre Workshop's *O, What a Lovely War* (1963). But while subsuming canonical writers into the world of the fiction made it possible to engage directly with the cultural texts of public, historical memory, this device also amplified the problem of repetition. Barker takes her place in a line of writers on twentieth-century war who have wrestled with the problem of belatedness, as did the Second World War poet Keith Douglas when writing about his Great War poet-hero Isaac Rosenberg in 'Desert Flowers': 'Rosenberg I only repeat what you were saying' (Douglas, 102). One of the ways Barker has escaped what Douglas called the 'tautological', repeating the same notion in different words, is by creating a network of dialogues in which experience and its interpretation in language are held up for examination and 'transformation' (a term used by the psychotherapist W. H. R. Rivers). The most obvious of these are internal to the novel's fictional world, notably the analytic encounter between doctor and patient, but another important dialogue is the one set up with the reader's existing cultural experience of the war.

The novelist and critic Geoff Dyer has argued that contemporary novelists working with this national memory are doomed not only to repetition, but to derivativeness: 'The problem with many recent novels about the war is that they almost inevitably bear the imprint of the material from which they are derived, can never conceal the research on which they depend for their historical and imaginary accuracy' (Dyer, 79). But Dyer also thinks 'it has become impossible to see the war except through the words of Owen and Sassoon,' or through Paul Fussell's 'ground-breaking investigation and collation of its dominant themes' in his book of literary and cultural criticism, *The Great War and Modern Memory*, published in 1977 (Dyer 77, 84). These two claims, one about the tendency of novelists to buttonhole us with the fruits of their research, the other about the difficulty of distinguishing the past from our most prized representations of it, actually help us see just what it is that Barker has achieved in *Regeneration*. They also suggest why her name might now be added to the list of those authors whose vision mediates the Great War to us with the explanatory power of myth. We will see again and again how the form of Barker's trilogy transforms her materials, as well as our relation to them as members of a historicized culture. This is the case with her use of social and cultural history, as well as with her literary allusions (though when we come to consider these in detail it will become apparent that repetition carries a different charge in different contexts).

A prime example of the reciprocity of content and form is the way that the Freudian analytic hour, and the place of transference in psychoanalysis (that is the way the patient displaces feelings about others onto the analyst, or repeats earlier relationships in analysis), becomes the template of the novels' most fundamental dramatic device, the dialogic encounter in which characters reveal an openness to an exchange of viewpoints. Barker's fiction achieves a 'constructive agency' in its presentation of conflicting themes and perspectives: this phrase was used by W. H. R. Rivers, in his revisions of Freud's theory of dreams, referring to his heterodox idea that dreams, rather than fulfiling wishes, were attempts at solving conflicts (Rivers, *Conflict*, 49). But in the case of fiction which deals with history as well as fantasy, this constructive agency is manifest in the preservation of contradiction, not in its resolution.

Barker's presentation and interpretation of the Great War is distinctive when compared with the canonical writing about the war from 1914 to 1930; this itself is an important dimension of the cultural 'compulsion to repeat', and of taking guard against tautology. Where much war literature insists on the divisions between the theatres of war and the home front (Remarque and Sassoon contributed to the figuration of war experience as something incommunicable to civilians), Barker creates a panoptic account, and one in which the divisions between front line and home front are permeable. This permits juxtapositions which disturb the categories (legal, moral and ideological) through which we reproduce our social reality: for example the courage of women who are the majority victims of domestic violence is held up alongside the endurance of soldiers in the ironic claim that 'Peace broke out' on 4 August 1914, when husbands went off to war (Regeneration, 110). This unusual capacity to connect acts of violence, which are normally kept separate by their differential legitimacy and visibility, is one of the continuities between this phase of Barker's writing, and her books of the 1980s, but the new, national historical context gives this device a further resonance.

Another distinction is that the protagonist of Regeneration lacks the authority of front-line, combatant experience; having a therapeutic hero, W. H. R. Rivers, the novel reappraises the hostility to the medical profession we sometimes find in war literature (the doctor in Owen's Craiglockhart poem 'The Dead Beat', his first attempt at imitating the style of Sassoon, dismisses a neurasthenic soldier as 'scum', and has therefore become an emblem of professional indifference for generations of readers). Through this revaluation of non-combatant experience, Barker acknowledges that the social dimensions of the war were larger than much of the canonical literature suggests. Other devices for democratizing the war include the use to which Rivers's anthropological perspectives are put in The Ghost Road, and the productive anachronisms (particularly the importation of late twentieth-century attitudes to self, sexuality and class) which are generated through the character of Billy Prior. We can summarize by calling Barker's imagined Great War a revisionist historical construct, which deliberately counters extant visions of the war to reveal a secret history, the dimensions of 1914–18 which have been overlooked because of the different pressures created by official remembrance, the literature of protest, and an abiding strain of popular militarism in Britain, as well as because of presumption or prejudice. But as a work of fiction it is more than a contribution to the renewal of historical images in the light of contemporary research, values and needs. Regeneration and its sequels represent a substantial development in the complexity and aesthetic power of Barker's writing about violence and its social meanings.

REGENERATION

The first words of *Regeneration* are not Barker's but Sassoon's, his 'A Soldier's Declaration' with its avowal that the author is 'Finished with the War'. On one level, we can read the novel as a para-text to Sassoon's famous fictionalized memoirs of the Great War, collectively known as *The Memoirs of George Sherston* (1928–36). Sassoon's carefully plotted trilogy offered an account of how its author swapped his bellicose enthusiasm for hostility to British military strategy, but it does so only by suppressing its author's identity as a poet (Barker also draws directly on Sassoon's later, straighter autobiography of the poet in wartime and after, *Siegfried's Journey*, published in 1945). Sassoon did write about his treatment under Rivers, but he offered only an apologetic version of Remarque's idea that the hospital was a symbol of the reality of war: 'Although a shell-shock hospital might be described as an epitome of the after-affects [*sic*] of the "battle of life" in its most unmitigated form, nevertheless while writing about Slateford [his disguise for Craiglockhart] I suffer from a shortage of anything to say' (Sassoon, 644–5). *Regeneration* supplies imaginatively what Sassoon longed for: 'I would give a lot for a few gramophone records of my talks with Rivers' (Sassoon, 636). The reciprocity between fiction and earlier documents reveals itself in both convergences and divergences; *Regeneration* treats them as sources but also as objects in an interrogation of values.

The story of Sassoon and Rivers, his therapist, provides *Regeneration* with its overarching narrative trajectory. This involves an ironic reversal (Sassoon is eventually discharged for general service overseas), a reversal and hence critique of the intended outcomes of the therapeutic encounter, and also a rhetorical reversal, the plot taking the form of a chiasmus (from the Greek for a crossing or diagonal arrangement). Put bluntly, Sassoon comes to accept Rivers's argument that his protest has made him immune to war's harms, safe among those whose complacence and lack of imagination he arraigns (36). Meanwhile, Rivers becomes uncomfortably aware of how far his own beliefs have been shifted in talking Sassoon out of his. While Rivers is 'in conflict with the authorities', Sassoon has apparently found a 'solution' to the conflict between his opposition to the war and his wish to return to France (249). This exchange is prefigured in the writings of both Sassoon and Rivers. Rivers, analyzing his own dreams in his posthumous book *Conflict and Dream* (1923), a critique of Freud's *The Interpretation of Dreams* (1900), recalls considering the possibility that 'my task of converting a patient from his "pacifist errors" to the conventional attitude should have at its result my own conversion to his point of view'. He is struck by the 'humorous side of the imagined situation' and concludes that it was a 'good opening for conflict and repression' manifested in his dreams (Rivers, 168, 32). Sassoon's version recalls that 'one of our jokes had been about the humorous situation which would arise if I were to convert him to my point of view', the verbal echoes of Rivers's text suggesting Sassoon had consulted it while writing his own memoirs (Sassoon, 661).

What are the possibilities for reinterpreting twentieth-century apocalypse via this 'humorous' situation? Much is suggested by Ruth Head's remark to Rivers in *Regeneration*: 'You want perception, you go to a novelist, not a psychiatrist' (164). Awareness or recognition is antithetical to the military, no matter how important in the art of war. It is certainly not required of any subaltern: 'What's he want insight for? He's supposed to be killing the buggers, Rivers, not psychoanalysing them' (245). Nor is it conducive to the aims of military medicine. Moreover, the distinction between story-teller and therapist makes playfully explicit a juxtaposition which will be the hallmark of Barker's fiction through the 1990s and beyond. An ironical treatment of therapeutic expertise is a prominent device in her probing of how our culture works through the violence of the twentieth century. Barker dramatizes discourses which have been developed to make sense of deviations from the modern goals of civil existence, from the treatment of 'shell shock' to the diagnosis of personality disorders. The representations of human harm, value and order to which these therapeutic disciplines have given rise are constelled by Barker into narratives which are open to contradictions, aporia and paradox.

What is it that novelists can perceive – that is be aware of, recognize or even intuit – that doctors who treat the symptoms of mental illness cannot? Rivers's psychoanalytic methods are distinguished by their humanity from some of the psychiatric therapies represented in *Regeneration*: indeed psychoanalysis is routinely contrasted with psychiatry in terms of an aspiration to understanding and treating causes, rather than symptoms (Schwartz, 2). But above all it is the talking cure, the analytic hour, which is the most important analogue linking Rivers's insights with the novel's power to generate cognitive and critical perspectives. This is not to suggest that Rivers is a cognitive hero, a cipher for the novelist. Indeed, the novel may be thought of as cloaking too ready a knowingness on the character's part with the device of Rivers's glacially slow integration of his compartmentalized academic and affective life.

As we have seen, the story told by *Regeneration* is one of transference in the most literal and unprofessional sense, as Sassoon and Rivers swap places. The doctor comes under the influence of the treacherous convictions of the patient whose own conviction in them is progressively weakened. But the novel's resonance and eclecticism, its apparent power to displace other representations of the Great War, lies in its multiplying the instances and vectors of dialogue, in the manner of a latter-day Dostoyevsky under the description of Bakhtin: 'a *plurality of consciousnesses, with equal rights and each with its own world,* combine but are not merged in the unity of the event' (Bakhtin, 6). The most important of these dialogues pair Rivers with the imaginary Prior, and Sassoon with the all too famous Wilfred Owen.

As we have seen, the novel opens with a citation, Sassoon's declaration that the war is being prolonged unnecessarily: his diagnosis as a neurasthenic is a cover up, a way of discrediting his mutinous claim that the soldiers in France are being deceived as to Britain's war aims. The madness of the war is encapsulated in the fact that speaking the truth about the madness of the war can get you declared insane. This is the ironical territory which Joseph Heller decisively named in *Catch-22* (1961). In *Beware of Pity* (1939), the Austrian novelist and pacifist Stefan Zweig has his protagonist argue that 'It always demands a far greater degree of courage for an individual to oppose an organized movement . . . . During the war practically the only courage I came across was mass courage' (15). In these and other respects, Sassoon is the antithesis of Rivers's usual patients. For a start, his poems witness a 'determination to remember', not the effort to forget trauma which 'precipitated . . . neurosis' in the typical officer-inmate of Craiglockhart (25–6). Indeed he appears to have a 'very powerful *anti*-war neurosis', an idea which Barker derives from Sassoon's phrase 'anti-war complex', complex being an item of folk-psychoanalytic jargon which Rivers deliberately avoided using (Sassoon, 632; Rivers, *Instinct*, 97).

The diagnosis is a kind of joke, but one which, as with many jokes, is a response to real conflicts, and which opens up heterodox perspectives on military values. Sassoon's presence has the additional effect of politicizing medicine, of revealing the Hippocratic dilemma of the military therapist. For how is the process of healing compatible with the vow to attend to 'the good of the patient' if it ends in the patient's return to the front? This point holds good even when we acknowledge that only a small minority of mind-shattered patients were returned to military duty in 1917 (Shepherd, 83). Sassoon's 'horror' is not a psychological reaction, but has been integrated into a (unacceptable) political stance; his poems are a form of unwitting self-therapy, in which recreating the front for purposes of anti-war propaganda has acted as a counter to defensive repression. Rivers realizes that the task of changing Sassoon's mind, of getting him to disown the declaration, could have the effect of making him ill, of 'precipitating a relapse' of nightmares and hallucinations (26).

In the process, Rivers will develop all the characteristic symptoms of a 'war neurosis' of his own: 'I already stammer and I'm starting to twitch' (140). By the close of the novel, 'the sheer extent of the *mess* seemed to be forcing him into conflict with the authorities over a very wide range of issues ... medical, military' (249). Sassoon, whose protest is made increasingly untenable by the very facts of the war's prolongation and his hospitalization, has been boarded for General Service Overseas.

The plot thus enacts a fantasy evinced in poems by both Sassoon and Owen, the fantasy that those who knew nothing of the Front Line could be shocked out of their 'complacence' (Sassoon's term in his declaration) by the power of poetry. Owen would subsequently claim that such compassion or Pity was the only legitimate manifestation of Poetry in this war. Rivers has come to function as 'substitute father' (145) to Sassoon. However Barker's allusions to Owen's retelling of the story of Abraham's sacrifice of Isaac (his parable about the liquidation of male youth by Europe's patriarchs) underlines the way that Rivers is nevertheless detached from the party of the Fathers in his 'rebellion of the old' (249).

Barker has made out of Rivers a diviner of 'the paradoxes of the war' (107), a self-aware and increasingly critical observer of the way in which the war undoes one's most fundamental convictions. A paradox is counter-orthodoxy; as Thomas DeQuincey wrote '[a] paradox . . . is simply that which contradicts the popular opinion – which in too many cases is the false opinion' (De Quincey, vol. 4, 73). But this non-technical sense – a proposition that appears absurd, counter-intuitive, self-contradictory or just surprising – underplays the most challenging aspect of the phenomenon: for a paradox involves the dilemma of non-integration. One cannot accept everything that looks acceptable or reasonable in a paradox; there appears to be a clash between acceptable principles and one of them must go. Paradox is a particularly apposite term for describing a dialogic fiction about psychotherapy, for paradoxes, unlike contradictions, may be resolved (e.g., it may turn out that there isn't really a contradiction, or that one of the premises is not true). One of the most influential literary-critical statements about paradox is the claim made in the 1940s by Cleanth Brooks that paradox is the particular language of poetry. This idea draws notably on Coleridge's theory that the imagination is the mental faculty which achieves the 'balance or reconcilement of opposite discordant qualities' (Coleridge, vol. 2, 14). Paradox, in this sense, is a marker of the non-logical in literary language, and it is manifested in linguistic ambiguity, irony and connotation, in multiple meanings and the tensions between them.

In Sassoon's case the paradox is 'like being three different people', the sportsman, the aesthete, 'and then the war' (35). Presently what he cannot integrate is his rational refusal to continue a war 'deliberately prolonged' (3) and his duty as subject of an ethos of military masculinity. This division is symbolized in his desecration of his uniform (tearing off the ribbon of the Military Cross) and by his sense of the stigma of being a neurasthenic patient, a coward in the eyes of the world (he hasn't a wound stripe). He'd hated Germans, and now he hates civilians (with whom, having expelled himself from the army, he has joined numbers).

The paradox Rivers seizes on concerns the subalterns' paternal care for his men, a duty which literary history has tended to see as the reason why Sassoon and Owen determined to return to active service, and to killing, in Flanders. But Barker complicates this further, bringing out the tension between agency and conformity in Sassoon and Owen, by redefining the gender of war itself. The fictional Rivers gradually uncovers one of the subtexts to war neurosis (which were elaborated by Showalter in the 1980s), and builds it into a theory of the origins of war neurosis which connects military and civil experience. War neurosis is, in a sense, domestic, feminine neurosis sent abroad, rather as, echoing Shakespeare's *Henry V*, war is the exporting of domestic violence (222). War which 'promised so much in the way of "manly" activity had actually delivered "feminine" passivity' (108–9). This conflict between actuality and expectation can be folded into Rivers's revisions of Freud, and his explanation for breakdown. While the reader's sense of the salience of this perspective owes much to late twentieth-century discourses about gender wholly antithetical to those which dominated British culture at the time of the war (when some suffragists suspended their campaign for the vote for the duration of hostilities), it is also apparent that these meanings were in circulation in texts about the war. R. C. Sherriff's hit West End play of 1928, *Journey's End*, is a classic, though veiled, rendition of this womanly front-line masculinity. In the play, which studiously codes mental breakdown as alcoholism, scenes involving the care of one male for another are repetitions of peacetime relationships between the characters – pupil–teacher, prefect–new boy – which substitute for the absent mother. Barker's feminization of attributes coded exclusively masculine – for instance, puttees are brilliantly compared to stays when Sarah tries to undress Prior (216) – extends then to the idea of the paternal officer and therapist (a 'substitute father'), who now appears as a '*male mother*' (145, 107). Rivers is made uneasy by the idea that the warrior male is being domesticated by a war of attrition. His anthropological imagination interprets the process as an equivalent of *couvade* or 'hatching', primitive customs in which men ape childbirth: what goes unstated here is a further sub-text, the term's survival in the derisive phrase, *faire la couvade* 'to sit cowring or skowking within dores, to lurke in the campe when Gallants are at the Battell' (*OED*).

Barker amplifies the process by which Rivers detaches himself from the bellicist convictions into which he was educated by attributing to the character a set of speculations about modern military masculinity which chime with the themes of gender studies. Showalter had led the way in recasting the Great War as 'a crisis of masculinity and a trial of the Victorian masculine ideal' (171). Another apparently anachronistic move in the design of this historical fiction is the figure of Billy Prior. Barker has acknowledged that this character was invented as a provocation to Rivers (Monteith, 2002, 72), not least because he perceives the doctor's sexual ambivalence. As well as his bisexuality, Prior's working-class background provides another way of reconfiguring the 'archive' of the Great War (Hitchcock, 2002, 9). Particularly in its literary dimension, the public memory of the war is dominated by the figure of the 'temporary gentleman', the officer enlisted for the duration. Prior presents as a mute, which is an aberration because officers usually display a different class of symptom, they stammer. Barker turns the data of military psychiatry into a figure for the reification of class, reminding us that war literature has been a major factor in the preservation of the figure of the gentleman as hero (and this is despite the circulation of two contradictory myths about the military in the world wars, one about the incompetence of the regular officer class in the Great War, the other about the democratization of the military in the 'People's War' of 1939–45).

Few canonical texts represent the experience of the other ranks other than through the mouthpiece of the educated subaltern: the Australian Frederic Manning's *Her Privates We* (1930) is a notable exception. In *Regeneration*, after Rivers has witnessed Yealland's brutal restoration of Private Callan's voice with the use of an electric current, he analyzes his own conflicted identification with regimes of control which have the effect of silencing 'the recalcitrant' (again a parallel with the scold's bridle factors in the issue of gender), that is of regenerating docile men: Sassoon's abandoning his protest comes to mind. (The metaphor of regeneration was applied to 'social hygiene' or national demographic fitness, in inter-war discourses about 'regenerating Britain' (Mark Harrison, 6)). Typically, Rivers's self-analysis is a means by which Barker can make explicit the very analogies which a rational analysis drawing on twentieth-century critiques of gender, class and representation would root out of the contradictions of the war. But here the scenario points to a further analogy which escapes the analyst. Yealland and Rivers both occupy the position filled by Frank Wright, the parroting spiritualist, and Wilfred Owen, the pleader who speaks for the men who serve under him, 'watching their sufferings that I may speak of them as well as a pleader can' (Owen, *Letters*, 351). They form part of the cultural system which produces discourse for and about the inarticulate fallen.

Prior, then, represents a certain resistance to the cultural take-over of the memory of the Great War, the way in which public memory is relayed through texts by and about the officer class. That this is achieved in the device of Prior's resistance to Rivers's therapeutic techniques has manifold significance. Barker would fully develop her sceptical reflection on therapeutic discourses, as well as her inquiry into representations of violence, in the books she wrote after the trilogy. But in the immediate context, it is the fact that Rivers's Freudian conceptions of mental health are historical, rooted in a view of the psyche as constituted in experience (in contrast with Yealland's organic theory in which some pre-existing degeneracy leads to breakdown), that presents opportunities for making metaphorical connections between psychiatric approaches to war experience and the ways in which a culture deals with the crises and disasters in its past. Bound up with memory and forgetting, and with regimes of regenerative remembering, Prior's analytical treatment, during which he presumes to answer back and swap places with the analyst, constantly invokes other memorial practices, and the idea that repression can operate in relation to inconvenient facts as well as painful memories.

The character of Prior brings into focus the relationship between conscious knowledge and unconscious processes. He is literally prior in his rational pre-emption of the discourse of others. Sassoon and Owen discuss the adequacy of the emblem of the soldier as Christ (which figures prominently in the poetry of each) with its implication of trench pacifism. But Prior has previously pointed out that the figure of the crucified Christ has already been appropriated by the military as the name for a field punishment (Barker has Prior overinterpret the shackling of soldiers as a propaganda error, which is a clever way of simultaneously pointing to the prominence of crucifixion motifs in propaganda stories about German atrocities). Prior is also always anticipating Rivers, entering into analysis sceptically forearmed with conceptual presumptions about 'negative transference' (65), or turning the analysis back onto the older man's history, when he notes that the fact that Rivers stammers is more interesting than the fact that he, Prior, does not.

But Prior's verbal and cognitive power is dramatically counter-pointed with an absence of awareness, a repression which has produced silence, and which is associated in *The Eye in the Door* with what might today be called a multiple-personality disorder. This repression also produces narrative suspense and plays on the reader's fascination with abomination – what is it that was so bad that Prior presented these symptoms, and cannot remember – in contrast to the many other cases which the narrative details in an inventory of traumatic experience and taboo-challenging representation.

Barker uses this narrative of discovery to complicate the question of attitudes to war, revealing Prior to be both a mocker of establishment values and a warrior male. While the novelist and critic Adrian Caesar has rooted the contradictions in the war poets' attitudes to violence in a historically specific homosocial cult of suffering in English public schools (Caesar, 1993), Barker launches a broader prognosis which takes in both past and present representations of war as a good. Prior ridicules the military's denial of the realities of static, attrition warfare but shares their thrill at the heroic gesture – 'Boldly they rode and well . . . . Into the mouth of hell' – as instanced in an example of a once potent tradition of war poetry, Tennyson's 'The Charge of the Light Brigade' (1864) (66). Prior's 'bloody-minded' offensiveness towards superiors is matched by his aggressive blood lust (101).

Just how contradictory attitudes to war can cohabit in the same personality is a theme Barker explores in all her characters. Rivers's scientific detachment, which Prior finds so unbearable in their analytic exchanges (exchanges that seem to him to be one way traffic in the unearthing of what is inside) is made analogous with Prior's own detachment from the memories he does recover (79). The writing of poetry, too, is figured as a kind of detachment, a way of controlling or achieving distance from traumatic experience. Yet to write against war is not to get beyond it: 'What's an anti-war poet except a poet who's dependent of war?' (*Eye*, 259).

In the pairing of the scientist and the soldier, the physician and the officer, Barker brings to the fore the question of the commissioning of pain (Rivers's notion of the feminized, passive soldier reflects the technological and tactical conditions of the Western

Front, but also a representational tradition which figures the Great War serviceman as primarily a target and victim, very rarely an aggressor). The public goods of experimentation and military psychiatry are juxtaposed with erotic satisfactions:

> 'you'd have to be *inhuman* to be as detached as that.'
>   'All right. It felt . . .' Prior started to smile again. '*Sexy.*' (78)

The way that the patient teasing out of ethical dilemmas is connected with the eruption of desire is responsible for our sense of recognition that we are not reading the same old thing in this narrative of war. Barker's version speaks to the intellectual and emotional needs revealed by our latter-day fascination with the Western Front.

It is at Prior's insistence that Rivers employs hypnosis (a therapy of last resort for Rivers) to 'recover lost memory' (68). What the change of method brings about is a change of narrative *mise-en-scène* to the trenches, and an episode derived closely from a passage in Edmund Blunden's much revised Flanders memoir *Undertones of War* (1928). Prior is as underwhelmed by what lies behind his memory loss – '*Is that all?*' – as some critics have been to discover Barker's debts, for instance Blunden's eyeball (104). Jung's concept of 'cryptomenesia' (hidden or secret memory) has been invoked to explain how the author could have believed she invented something that she had 'merely forgotten' (Whitehead, 68). But critical anxiety about plagiarism seems as misplaced as Prior's concern that he should have broken down over 'nothing' (that is handling the eyeball of a soldier he'd just been eye-to-eye with). There is a certain irony in the experience Prior cannot repeat being a literal repetition, admittedly one with some significant variations, of a canonical work of Great War witness (though as Paul Fussell first taught us, it is a mistake to presume that the authors of the famous Great War memoirs did not shape their material for aesthetic or economic ends). But more interesting is the fact that Barker's fictional practice is simultaneously open to the criticism that it departs from the historical record and that it parrots it.

This is particularly the case with Barker's high-risk incorporation of the person and the works of Wilfred Owen in the novel. Using Owen's words in an imaginative work was not itself new (the practice was inaugurated by the greatest English poet of the century, W. H. Auden, in *The Orators* of 1932). Anticipating Barker's hospital scenario, Stephen MacDonald had drawn on Owen's letters in his play *Not About Heroes*. This two-hander about Sassoon and Owen at Craiglochhart was premiered at the 1982 Edinburgh Festival in the wake of Falklands militarism (its title derives from a draft preface Owen composed for the collection of poems he didn't live to publish). It has since been revived for performance at such war-heritage sites as the Imperial War Museum (in the building in Southwark which housed 'Bedlam', the earliest psychiatric hospital, until 1930) and the Cabinet War Rooms. MacDonald drew attention to the mixture of citation and invention he'd employed to 'refresh the memory' of the two poets, an expressly Owen-like mission (MacDonald, Author's Note). Barker's acknowledgements too claim to clear up sources: 'Fact and fiction are so interwoven in this book that it may help the reader to know what is historical and what is not' (251). But this underplays what arises from the book's 'interweaving', which is a new constellation of the elements which are repeated in the public history of the Great War (primarily in school and on television).

Barker draws on Owen's writing to recreate him, but also to create the contexts in which the other characters are fleshed out. Before Owen is introduced in person, sheepishly seeking an audience with the published author Siegfried Sassoon, his writing has surfaced in a description of bathing: the chlorinated water, and the description of the 'green, silent world' into which Sassoon dives explicitly invoke 'Dulce et decorum est', Owen's well-known poem about a poison gas attack. Rivers's efforts to get Prior to overcome his detachment results in a recollection of going over the top which centres on 'an amazing sense of exultation', the last word being the key to Owen's less anthologized 'Apologia pro poemate meo', with its celebration of the 'glee' of soldiers as 'we slashed bones bare' (Owen, *Poems*, 101).

By contrast with Prior's discourse of war (in which the full implications of the coupling of sexuality and violence are exploited), the narrative presents Wilfred Owen's efforts to give expression to the war as comparatively genteel, both for their content and in relation to Sassoon's insistence that poetry is a kind of 'drill' or discipline (125). There is something more troubling about this than the usurpation of the literary record for the purposes of make believe. *The Eye in the Door* returns to the idea of a 'suffering competition' (70, 101), the way that the very act of telling your story issues in a hierarchy of entitlement to sympathy. The trilogy's adaptation of its historical sources is aimed at unravelling the hierarchy (with the combatant male not at the base but the apex) that a canon of war literature has helped establish. But the adaptation of the literary record seems to introduce another competition, this time a competition for authority. The trilogy feeds off this apparent rivalry between witness and historical novelist, in particular through its promotions and demotions of the fictional and the real, and its refusal to observe the courtesies of attribution. But in the end, it comes down to a question of transference, and of the gap between the narrative and the needs that are projected onto it. In recent years military historians have complained that a predominantly anti-war poetry has become the major historical source in public knowledge of the Great War, and an unrepresentative one at that. But the poetry take-over has been proceeding for some time. We can see it going on in the way Richard Attenborough's film *Oh! What a Lovely War* (1969) replaces the trench newspaper the 'Wipers Gazette' (based on the historical *Wipers Times*, written and printed by soldiers in the Ypres sector) cited in Theatre Workshop's stage play *Oh, What a Lovely War* (1963), with a poem by Rupert Brooke. Anonymous, ephemeral discourse is substituted by a legendary, even a celebrity voice. Barker's historical fiction feeds off this homage and yet counteracts it. Her dramatization of the revision of 'Anthem for Doomed Youth', drawing on Owen's letters, as well as surviving manuscripts which reveal the way the two poets worked to refine the vocabulary and the sense of the sonnet, is a case in point. 'Anthem' has divided critics for generations. This is notably because its concluding sestet, through tropes like 'each slow dusk a drawing-down of blinds', seems to reintroduce the religiose sentiments (akin to spiritualism's metaphysics of denial) which the opening octet dismisses as euphemistic and therefore insulting memorials to the servicemen who have been slaughtered 'like cattle', as the last state of the poem has it. The dialogue here may tell us nothing new about how the poem's meanings are achieved, but it does restore a sense of labour and contingency to a body of poetry Seamus Heaney has compared to 'martyr's relics' (Heaney, xiv). The idea of bringing an Owen 'ungrounded by war' back down to earth – the theme of Brock's ergotherapy which Owen represents allegorically in his poem on Hercules and Antaeus (123) – is taken further in *The Ghost Road*. Prior, having escaped from a séance in Sarah's home town, makes to close the curtains so they can take advantage of Ada's absence: 'No, don't do that, they'll think somebody's dead. Behind the sofa' (*Ghost*, 80). This joke on the pathetic fallacy at the close of 'Anthem for Doomed Youth' encapsulates the scandal of putting Owen's words into the mix with those of the novelist's characters (a Bakhtinian levelling). If Barker's novels are novels of character and not novels of ideas, as she has claimed (Monteith, 2004, 31–2), this practice is a clue to how her narratives keep ideas and their implications in motion.

THE EYE IN THE DOOR

Having published *Regeneration*, Pat Barker stated in interview that she wanted to write a sequel which would be about two aspects of the war that came into focus as a result of using Craiglockhart in 1917 as a lens on the war: the fate of non-conformists in wartime society, and what the war poets *weren't* saying. As represented in *The Eye in the Door*, the former are deviants from the dominant ideology of warrior masculinity that it was necessary for the state and its subjects (both male and female) to reproduce and act out if they were to continue to prosecute the war into 1918, in particular, pacifists and homosexuals. At the same time Barker is suggesting that we should think of Sassoon and Owen as conforming; despite the well-established tradition of reading them as anti-war poets they are identified as warrior males who 'enjoyed' war (Nixon, 19).

It is now easier to read Sassoon and Owen against the grain of their reception, which had tended to dissolve the contradictions between the positive values they associated with soldiering and their negation of the war. Nowadays we can seek to understand these contraries as aspects of a long-range transformation of the social and cultural significance of warfare in Britain. *Regeneration* presented Sassoon as an officer acutely conscious of his reputation for bravery, and drawn back to the *comitatus* of the trenches, one who is angered by the way the war is being prolonged, but who is committed to the shared experience of war. But the meanings of these emotions – especially the offensive aggression for which Sassoon was famed – are more fully explored through the

analysis of Prior. Barker appears reluctant to reinvent her historical characters: she acknowledged that where Rivers was 'a blank
screen' on which to 'project', Owen came with 'his own preexisting myth' (Stevenson, 176). It is no surprise that the character of
Billy Prior is the vehicle for countering this apparent suppression
of the joy of war. There will be more to say about Prior shadowing,
or converging on, Owen when we come to *The Ghost Road*.

The Eye in the Door has its germ in the idea of pressures towards
conformity, and its ruling metaphor is taking sides. This figure
serves to interweave a psychiatric plot and a political plot (echoing the novel genre's perennial interest in the struggle between
individualism and conformity in the reproduction of the social
order). It also provides an analogical framework for reflecting
on war enthusiasm in its social and libidinal dimensions. The
war poets made much of contradictions in the adversary thinking which was mandated by wartime propaganda; us *versus* them,
the Christian English against the barbaric Hun. Scandalously, the
front-line troops of the Allied and the Central powers could be
represented by these poets as having more in common with each
other, and with their junior officers, than with civilians in London
or Berlin. But the rhetoric of sides in *The Eye in the Door* owes as
much to Prior's attempted disruption of the analytic relationship
with Rivers: '"I had been rather assuming we were on the same
side".... "I had been *rather assuming* that we were not"' (*Regeneration*, 80). The mocking impersonation of the doctor is a blow in
the Oedipal struggle with Rivers, and a challenge to the authority
of the therapeutic institution, as well as a negation of propaganda
about national unity, an emphasis on linguistic markers of class
to counteract the legend that 'there are no class distinctions at the
front' (*Regeneration*, 67).

As a sequel or continuation, *The Eye in the Door* literally revolves
around a repetition or return, the resumption of Prior's treatment by Rivers, whom he'd promised to look up only 'after the
war' (*Regeneration*, 210). Where the narrative of the earlier novel
was in part driven by suspending the revelation of what Prior
had repressed, in this one Rivers's repressed memories become
a secret we read in pursuit of (and discover only in *The Ghost
Road*). The eye of the title brings to mind Tower's eyeball, the
gob-stopper, or in psychoanalytic terms, the 'unknown' event, of
which Prior's mutism is a symptom (Caruth, 4). But the episode

now has a talismanic value for Prior: this recovered memory or 'belated experience' means '[t]here's no possible room for doubt where your loyalties are' (*Eye*, 70). The mouth has been substituted by the eye as the dominant figure for control in the narrative (Brannigan, 2002, 19). The eye is a symbol for the situation of being watched as well as for what you are forced to look upon: surveillance by jailors, surveillance by a patient, surveillance by the invention of conspiracies, guilty self-surveillance. The unearthing of plots against the state (Betty Roper's assassination of Lloyd George, Pemberton Billing's 'First 47,000') is a species of ideological disciplining, and it reveals the state at war to be a kind of fiction. The pretence of national unity is anxiously reproduced by unearthing threats to undermine it. Barker exploits this establishment paranoia to complicate assumptions about military and civilian life during the war, particularly those that issue from Sassoon's satire on home front indifference to the sufferings of the nation in France. As *The Eye in the Door* illustrates, it takes courage to be a pacifist, or to attend a performance of Oscar Wilde's play *Salome* or to lack the sense to '*shut up*' like Billy's battered mother (90), the most explicit connection to the narratives of female courage in the context of masculine monopoly over violence in *Union Street* and *Blow Your House Down* (we might recall Nicole Ward Jouve's remark that 'Victoria Crosses don't go to the right quarters').

Prior's background links the trilogy to the Northern England of the early novels, but so too does his familiarity with brutality. While Londoners recall the atrocity stories of 1914 – 'Nuns with their breasts cut off' – as Germans mount their 1918 Spring Offensive, Prior apprehends the capital in terms of its celebrity sex-murderer, Jack the Ripper. He tells Myra she's the 'sort of girl who ends in a ditch with her stockings round her neck'; the 'titless' Ministry girls 'woke his demons up' (5, 178). A 'fascination with the Ripper' persists despite the military carnage, and the Ripper is the figure Prior seizes upon to represent the activities of his dark side, repressed, he mockingly presumes, because they are as terrible as having '[n]ipped over to Whitechapel and ripped up a few prostitutes' (194, 132).

The Eye in the Door begins to tease out the relationship between the violence of fantasy, the violence which is going on abroad (Owen's poetry insists that only soldiers know what this is like) and the violence that has been going on, unacknowledged, behind closed doors in every street in England. Barker has stated explicitly her interest in what 'public violence and private violence' have in common, in the 'network' between 'legitimate public violence, domestic violence, and ... criminal violence outside the home' (Stevenson, 179–80). Part of the ideological work of our culture is, and long has been, to make these connections invisible. The state's monopoly over legitimate force is rendered intelligible by positive representations of military adventure (the pleasure culture of war), as well as by the denial of such descriptions to those who contest this monopoly (interned members of the IRA were denied the label 'prisoners-of-war', suicide bombers are 'cowards'). The sanctity of the home and the unimpeachable position of the father have until very recently helped create a categorical distinction between the force legitimately deployed to maintain authority through chastisement, and the criminal assault or rape performed by strangers (the first shelters for battered women were opened in the 1970s). The best evidence of the persistence of the latter distinction is the moral panic surrounding the abuse and murder of children, which invariably exaggerates the threat of strangers while underplaying the proportion of victims who are preyed upon or killed by family members. 'Murder', Rivers reflects in *The Ghost Road*, 'was only killing in the wrong place' (44).

Violence, then, is bound up with the terms of its representation. The material reality of pain is undeniable to the one experiencing it, but pain has no such obduracy in the cultural realm. Elaine Scarry has contrasted the facticity of experienced pain, which some contend is beyond the grasp of our expressive resources, with the facility with which the pain of others is 'redescribed' as something else, for instance a political good, such as victory (Scarry). We have noted how Prior's self-admonishment about being drawn into a 'suffering competition' points beyond the different modes of wartime hardship to the way in which historical and cultural traditions privilege some experiences (combatant valour, even after the bankruptcy of *la gloire*) while making others invisible. It is not so much a suffering competition, but a competition amongst representations, which is precisely why Pat Barker's intervention in the reproduction of the story of the Great War can strike some as a revelation, and others as a misrepresentation.

The Home Front in *The Eye in the Door* is not the scene of homogeneous jingoism and complacency which we find portrayed in the writing of Owen, Sassoon, Robert Graves and others. Rather it is a social world which is continuously dividing and reforming, in the interplay between radical groupings – unionized labour, pacifists – and the authority of political and financial interests. War complicates questions of sides. Hostilities are re-enacted on hospital wards, where staff harass conscientious-objectors conscripted to roles as porters (Barker here takes up a scenario first broached in Mary Renault's path-breaking 1953 novel of homosexuality in the Second World War, *The Charioteer*). In another internal splitting, proletarian soldiers, Prior insists, are not in sympathy with striking munitions workers; however this militarized division of a class brings in its train counter-revolutionary fantasies: 'I'm surprised you feel *quite* so much pleasure at the idea of the workers shooting each other' (111). This viewpoint on the notorious shortages and unreliability of munitions is itself a partial perspective on the unprecedented industrial output of ordnance in the later years of the war: in what senses were there too few explosions on the Western Front? It produces a representational dissonance, striking sparks of recognition when it clashes against more familiar ways of looking at the socio-economic network of wartime, for instance Sassoon's 'The Glory of Women': 'You love us when we're heroes . . . . You make us shells' (Sassoon, 1983, 100).

Sassoon's symbolic monopoly of protest is directly countered in the character of Betty Roper, who *does* end up in prison for her opposition to the war. The misrepresentation of her intentions during her trial contrasts with the ways in which Sassoon's act of desertion is hushed up through its redescription (by Graves and by the military) as pathological. What had seemed an outrageous mode of confinement and silencing in *Regeneration* now appears a mild form of coercion. The women's prison, like the corridors of Craiglockhart, is an uncannily crowded yet deserted place, homologous with No Man's Land.

The homosexual sub-text to the therapeutic narrative, again involving Sassoon, is transformed into a thematic programme in *The Eye in the Door*. On one side is Rivers's patient Manning, whom the bisexual Prior (taboo-breaker and side-switcher) picks up after he has ditched Myra. In the character of Manning, Barker extrapolates some of the hints in Sassoon's interwar memoirs about his relationship with the friend he won't name to Rivers, and whose death prompted his 'Mad Jack' offensiveness. On the other side is the homophobic M. P. Pemberton Billing. Alarmist denunciations of a fifth-column of prominent Britons working as German agents and held in a bondage of corruption and black-mail, are a symptom of the way war shifts existing categories (given that Barker makes the character a caricature of illiberal-ism, it is diverting to try to imagine how a different narrative could be constructed about a man who was the co-founder of the aeronautics enterprise that became Supermarine Aviation, the firm for which designer Basil Mitchell created the Spitfire, mechanical hero of the Battle of Britain and Leslie Howard's 1942 film *The First of the Few*). Rivers, the expert on repression, rea-sons, ironically, that it is the way that war cancels inhibitions that leads to the scapegoating of homosexuals: 'there's this enor-mous glorification of love between men, and yet at the same time it arouses anxiety' (156). Reaction and counter-reaction are here viewed from the anthropological perspective which will be elaborated in *The Ghost Road*, and which, in this era, was a lens through which writers like Joseph Conrad and T. S. Eliot examined modern life.

The 47,000 are the complement of Robert Ross's photographs of the war wounded (actually it was Owen who used this demon-stration on acquaintances) an arresting icon to drive home a message about what the war is really like. But whatever moral glosses are placed on conflict, it is also a source of pleasure: war, according to Rivers's citation of Freud, erodes inhibitions con-cerning the thrill of the kill. This exhilaration is ubiquitous in *The Eye in the Door*, and, as we have already seen, the political opposition of Allied and Central powers is insufficiently power-ful or legitimate a concept to channel all such energies into the kind of hatred for the official enemy encouraged by atrocity sto-ries. In many instances, the animus, be it sex, rivalry, revenge or correction, is directed against a supposed ally in the interna-tional conflict who is nevertheless represented as an enemy. A sig-nal example is Prior's reading of the *The Times*' casualty list in a London pub:

> [he] would have liked nothing better, at that moment, than for a tank to come crashing through the doors and crush everybody, the way

they sometimes crushed the wounded who couldn't get off the track in time. (122)

This is precisely modelled on Siegfried Sassoon's righteous-sounding revenge on jingo-civilians in the poem 'Blighters', where the idea of the author's opposition to the prosecution of the war is complicated by the desire to turn the Home Front into a battlefield.

Like *Regeneration*, *The Eye in the Door* works analogically. Rivers's network of patients continues to present an array of related and contrastive symptoms, each of which is a 'solution' to conflicts arising from the experience of warfare. Sassoon, Prior, Manners and the others each bring to light a paradox so jarring as to produce illness or its semblance. They are symbols of the war in the sense that their pathologies stand in the place of that event which was so traumatic that it could not be woven into the tissue of memory, and integrated into the value schemes by which each lived. In addition, *The Eye in the Door* presents a more panoramic vision of a society at war, and derives from its dramatization of the conflicts internal to that society what amounts to a socio-psychoanalytic model of war. Prior's insight into the workings of the secret state anticipates Rivers's account of scapegoating in grasping how, in wartime, reality seems loosed from its customary moorings:

> Not much grasp of reality in all this, Prior thought, on either side. He was used to thinking of politics in terms of conflicting interests, but what seemed to have happened here was less a conflict of interests than a disastrous meshing together of fantasies. (52)

What is true of Whitehall's intelligence branches is more broadly true of war considered as an exercise in wish-fulfilment, a collective dream. *The Eye in the Door* counterpoints the discourse of war's horrors explored in *Regeneration* with representations of its compensations: Prior's '*Standard issue battle nightmares*', accompanied by ejaculation, is the trilogy's primary emblem for this shaming combination of affects (*Regeneration*, 100). This perspective is a significant achievement on the novelist's part, for, in the same way that we inhabit a culture that makes some kinds of violence invisible, we are schooled to compartmentalize or dissociate these very different valuations of war, dismissing one as militarist, hallowing the other as liberal progress from militarism.

Dissociation is indeed the novel's other major theme, expanding on the treatment of detachment in *Regeneration*, and raising moral questions as well as issues about adaptation. Dissociation is, additionally, a metaphoric transmutation of the idea of sides. Prior, who is employed in intelligence because of his ability to cross from side to side class-wise, is usually a perspicacious commentator on adversarial relations. But he has blind spots: 'Do you *know* whose side you're on,' asks Betty Roper when he is telling himself that he's using his position at the Ministry to suborn its goals to help her (41). We only recognize the full implication of Betty's question when Prior is in session with Rivers again, and presents after an episode of memory loss: earlier he has mockingly interpreted his dream of the eye in the door as a guilty 'stabbing myself in the "I"' (75). Barker's particular interest in Prior's fugue state, beyond the suspensefulness of the pathological mystery, is in the kinds of investment that are made in such absences. These are represented by Prior's literary creation of a 'malignant double', and Rivers's scepticism about recovered memories. Prior's labelling his dissociated state as 'Hyde' (after Robert Louis Stevenson's *Dr Jekyll and Mr Hyde* of 1886) reflects a usage that was conventional by 1915, when the war correspondent Ian Hay alluded to Stevenson's characters in his account of the volunteers who made up Kitchener's New Army, *The First Hundred Thousand* (OED).

The renewal of Prior's treatment is also a resumption of his hostility towards the analyst. Again, we see Prior usurping Rivers's role, now pursuing the analyst's visual amnesia back towards childhood trauma. This is a canny device, on Barker's part, for Rivers in fact viewed the war as having saved the therapeutically valuable concepts of unconscious processes, and of forgetting – to him the valuable parts of Freud's work – from the resistance which was provoked by the Austrian's scandalous invocation of childhood sexuality as a root cause of the neuroses (Rivers, 1922, 4). The impact of Rivers's revision of Freud was to suggest that the importance of sexuality 'had been decisively disproved by wartime experience' (Shepherd, 87). Prior is used to challenge this parochialism, insisting that what Rivers has forgotten, and what accounts for his inability to remember visually, is rape (in *Regeneration*, Prior's resistance to treatment had involved inappropriately prurient interest in the sexual themes of Rivers's anthropological researches). But Rivers wants to preserve the idea of childhood terrors being distinct from, and probably insignificant from the perspective of, adult knowledge (this is a territory Barker had already explored in 'Kelly Brown').

Prior's interrogation provokes an introspective analysis in which Rivers traces a 'dissociation of personality' in his own make up (141). In Barker's hands this dissociation becomes a true analogy, a ratio which, through similitude, evokes comparable relationships or structures. The splitting of reason and emotion brings to mind the educational formation of English men (the militaristic cast of which is much in Virginia Woolf's mind in *Three Guineas*, her 1938 essay on war and gender), but also the nerve regeneration experiments of Henry Head. In *Regeneration*, experimental work is presented in the form of a dream, which Rivers interprets in terms of internal conflicts over his therapy: he aims to 'regenerate' soldiers, putting them back together again, by forcing them to 'abandon repression' (*Regeneration*, 48). But, indirectly, he is commissioning terrors. The labels Head and Rivers used to account for the difference in sensibility associated with two phases of the regeneration of nerve tissue, protopathic and epicritic, are associated in the novel with English middle-class masculinity (the repression of emotion), and with an evolutionary narrative of progress from the primitive to the sophisticated. The distinction is also tried out as an explanation of Sassoon's perplexing duality, 'Happy warrior one minute. Bitter pacifist the next' (*Regeneration*, 74). In *The Eye in the Door*, the repetition of the regeneration motif spells out some of these earlier analogies: 'both words had acquired broader meanings, so that "epicritic" came to stand for everything rational, ordered, cerebral, objective, while "protopathic" referred to the emotional, the sensual, the chaotic, the primitive' (*Eye*, 142). This process of broadening meaning is presented as both a cultural process (Rivers's thinking is, as it were, interrupted by the popularity of the *Jekyll and Hyde* 'shorthand for internal divisions') and as revelation of the inevitable, and potentially disastrous, circularity of any *science* of introspection: 'the experiment both reflected Rivers's internal divisions and supplied him with a vocabulary in which to express them' (142). Most importantly, from the perspective of Ruth Head's contrast between novelist and psychiatrists, this process is also a representation of the workings of the novel, which broadens meanings in the sense of making visible connections which otherwise escape us. What is convincing in the novel (a matter of the author's way with words) is very different to what is convincing in evidence-based science, which is why the novel can reach out for conclusions, even if it takes a third volume to arrive at one, while Rivers is left with the problem that Prior forces him to confront, namely the results of his rational, objective therapy, 'the ones who go back'. And to that challenge Rivers has only the scientific answer: 'Nobody's ever done a follow up' (205).

Rivers is in the position of the officer who commands his troops to go over the top. Manning's relationship with Scudder (the name of the gamekeeper in E. M. Forster's explicitly homosexual, pre-war but posthumously published novel *Maurice*) ratchets up the officer's responsibility for the enlisted man to the point of a mercy execution (there are echoes here of *All Quiet on the Western Front*, but also the Irish novelist Jennifer Johnston's powerful 1974 narrative *How Many Miles to Babylon?*). Scudder is a veteran of Yealland-style shell-shock treatment, and the source of one of Barker's best anti-therapist jokes – 'He dreamt he was back in the trenches having electric shock treatment' (169). As ineluctably as he is stuck in the mud of Flanders he is open to psychological insult or trauma by war, because he is unable to dissociate, to 'turn off the part of himself that minded' (170).

Barker's narrative will ultimately sustain Rivers's conviction that war has cleansed Freud's great insights of their sexual taint. In *The Ghost Road*, his childhood trauma is revealed to be the result of looking at a representation of warfare, the painting of Uncle William – the man who shot the man who shot Nelson – having his leg amputated, rather than an incidence of what we would now call sexual abuse. Barker provides this 'lesson in manliness' with a number of associations. The young William Rivers's entry into masculinity, screaming at having his hair cut short, and with his father pointing at the relative in the painting, is a version of the breeching scene (itself an echo of Lawrence's *Sons and Lovers*) from *Liza's England*. It resolves on an ostensive definition of manliness as repression: '*He didn't make a sound*'. But the painting is terrifying to the child: 'this is what happened to you if your name was William Rivers' (*Ghost*, 95). This repetition is coincidentally further coded in his name: William Halse Rivers (W. H. R.) Rivers.

The first information Burns volunteers about his service in France (triggered by the return of the Aldeburgh lifeboat with the Burril brothers on board) concerns the subaltern's responsibility for letters of condolence: 'suddenly you realize you've written the same name twice' (*Regeneration*, 182).

Dissociation becomes a metaphor for compartmentalization, for an inability to integrate the manifold dimensions of warfare. If this is one explanation of traumatic forgetting, it is also a description of how it is possible to hold contradictory values without confronting paradox. Sassoon's adaptation is explained, Rivers reasons metaphorically, by his 'being two people', protest poet and offensive company commander (*Eye*, 233). Prior's dissociated state is related verbally and thematically to Sassoon's changing conceptions of war. Charging along a German trench '[t]he old Sassoon had cracked wide open and something new had stepped out of the shell' (*Regeneration*, 115). Prior's double, who reminds Rivers of the antagonistic patient of the Craiglockhart days, 'was born . . . . [i]n a shell-hole in France', he is better at fighting, knows no fear (*Eye*, 240). But Prior's 'method of coping' is pathological, whereas Sassoon's is not. For the latter, 'experience gained in one state was available to the other': his 'experience of bloodshed supplied the moral authority for the pacifist's protest' (233). The trilogy is an attempt to multiply these channels between states of experience.

Understanding this permits us to make sense of the way Barker's narrative questions therapeutic discourses and her generosity towards Rivers's capaciousness of mind, despite the doubts he raises about his own practice. As Ben Shepherd has argued, in the context of the competing psychiatric responses to the high rates of breakdown amongst combatants, Rivers's technique was dependent on his personality, and it was debatable whether 'this method was replicable in other hands' (Shepherd, 87). Prior, notably, is unable to resist the counter-transference whereby patients get better to please the doctor, and additionally the character represents the dependence of Rivers's work on recruiting patients to self-analysis (Shepherd, 87). By the end of the sequel, Prior, the analyst-manqué, has to confront his ability at 'self-hypnosis', putting himself into a dissociated state in the repetition of a childhood 'way of dealing with a very unpleasant situation' (*Eye*, 248–9).

Rivers's objection to Prior's request for hypnosis is that in 'people who've dealt with a horrible experience by splitting it off from their rest of their consciousness', hypnosis reinforces a tendency to repeat that dissociation (*Regeneration*, 68). This aligns Rivers with late twentieth-century critiques of what Ian Hacking has called 'memory sciences' (Hacking, 209). Moreover, his doubts about the memories which are elicited by hypnosis – 'they can be fantasies, or they can be responses to suggestions from the therapist' – point beyond scepticism about the claims of psychotherapeutic expertise (the novel slyly alludes to the problem of the 'expert witness', the psychologists called in the Maud Allen libel case, thus anticipating *Border Crossing*) (*Eye*, 135). These doubts also model possible hostility towards the historical claims of fictions such as *The Eye in the Door*. For there are compelling parallels between therapy that revisits the past to bring to light what was 'not known in the first instance' (Caruth, 4) and fictional narrative which frames historical experience using concepts and values which were not available to participants.

It has been suggested that the formal diagnosis of post-traumatic stress disorder (PTSD) in 1980 in *DSM III* (the third edition of the *Diagnostic and Statistical Manual of Mental Disorders*) was a political artefact of the Vietnam anti-war movement (McNally, 1). That is to say, it was only within a particular framework of political assumptions about war, notably a rejection in the affluent Cold-War West of the idea that war can again involve the mass participation of ordinary citizens, that a group of symptoms could acquire the diagnostic authority and the medical reality that goes with inclusion in the *Manual*, the Bible of the mental health professions in the United States. Ian Hacking has examined the modern epidemic of multiple-personality disorder in a similar way, controversially advancing the view that a politicization of memory contributes to an iatrogenic pathology, that is one that is created by the practices, norms and institutions of medicine.

The nature of Prior's multiple-personality is of less consequence here than Rivers's sense that the splitting is iatrogenic: 'because most therapists are interested in dissociated states . . . they – unconsciously of course – encourage the patient further down that path' (*Eye*, 135). Hacking argues that the re-experiencing of the past which is central to conceptions of trauma – in the diagnostic dimension, the compulsion to repeat, and in the therapeutic, the restoration of lost memory – involves 'retroactive redescription'. It is of particular interest that his example is drawn not from the controversial recovery of memory in relation to childhood sexual abuse, but from the Great War, and specifically attempts to legislate pardons for soldiers executed for desertion or refusal to obey orders.

> The author of the private member's bill states that today the men would be judged to be suffering from post-traumatic stress disorder, and to be in need of psychiatric help, not execution. This is retroactive redescription with a vengeance . . . . It pathologizes old behaviour.
>
> (Hacking, 1995, 241)

Hacking interprets the bill as symbolic of an anti-war politics, but also notes that while it seems designed to 'save reputations', its retroactive redescription reduces the 'number of things that the soldiers might have done intentionally'; they can no longer choose – perhaps in an anti-war spirit like Sassoon's – to desert (ibid.). A contemporary understanding of war ironically results in the same pathologization that was meted out by the military authorities to silence a protest against the war in 1917.

But the real importance of this convergence between Hacking's investigation of the way social reality is constructed through the looping of categories and behaviour and Barker's reimagining of the Great War is in terms of the political and ethical consequences of retroactive redescription (Hacking, 2000). From Hacking's viewpoint, the past is indeterminate where we cannot avoid retroactive redescription, and this just comes with the territory of changing norms and concepts:

> I do not mean only that we change our opinions about what was done, but that in a certain logical sense what was done itself is modified. As we change our understanding and sensibility, the past becomes filled with intentional actions that, in a certain sense, were not there when they were performed.
>
> (Hacking, 1995, 249–50)

Redescriptions are neither correct nor incorrect; they are better understood as a political tactic which might usefully 'impose a new awareness' as they change the past (Hacking, 1995, 243).

To similar effect, Cathy Caruth, who has written influentially about the interplay between theories of trauma and literature, refers to a history 'which is not straightforwardly referential', one which is 'resituate[d] . . . in our understanding' (Caruth, 11).

These discussions are particularly apt in relation to a mode of historical writing which foregrounds the make-believe of characters with intentional states, and which, as is the case with the trilogy, blurs the distinction between its characters and historical figures. By shaping Prior's consciousness through the published words of Sassoon and Owen, and by ascribing to these historical figures intentions to mean something in excess of their already ambivalent literary records, Barker has created a narrative representation which simultaneously draws on the historical archive and makes a virtue of refracting it through the preoccupations of later generations. This may not satisfy some as the truth about the war, but it does mean that Barker comes closer than anyone to constellating the elements which make up the war of our understanding, the perennially repeated, and revised, symbol of an event that can never be assimilated enough. Cathy Caruth has defined trauma as 'the narrative of belated experience', the experience that could not be known at the time (Caruth, 7). But this would also be a good description of the trilogy, which could be considered in this context a form of belated vicarious experience.

Barker's narrative is busy with analogies and parallels, and the richness of the writing is evidenced by the fact that it is hard to draw a line where the analogies stop. There are certain parallels, for instance, between conspiracy theories, such as Pemberton Billing's (which propose events are caused by secret and deceptive plotters) and psychoanalysis (with its hidden, encrypted past causes of present symptoms). The narrative that brings these parallels to light is itself in the business of drawing on that which is secreted, overlooked. Does it then share the same kind of authority as the discourses of conspiracy and psychoanalysis (each of which has its passionate evangelists, and its equally righteous detractors)? A clue to how we should answer this question lies in the character of Rivers, who we see persisting in an effort to achieve an adequate response to the conflicts that arise between what he knows and what is happening. While the narrative of paradox and analogy generates a vertiginous sense of 'the vastness of war, the impossibility of one mind encompassing it all',

Rivers's capacity to move between the already porous compart-ments of his professional life constitutes a privileged holism. His doubts provide rhetorical support to this function.

Barker has talked about Rivers as working with a therapy with-out rules: 'He was trained as a neurologist, he's practising psy-chiatry, he calls himself a psychologist, and the divisions between these fields were simply not there' (Garland, 195). From this point onwards, the trilogy is increasingly concerned with aspects of his work in the field of anthropology which bear on the European situation. This constellation of disciplines is also a nomadic condi-tion; he is at home in none, and hence inoculated against compla-cence. In his arguments with the evidential basis of psychology, Hacking employs the figure of the anthropologist as a rhetorical alien, that is an investigator whose questions are supposedly not shaped by self-interest and the wish to demonstrate the objectiv-ity of his own discipline (Hacking, 100). This is a generous view of the anthropological disciplines, but it suggests why Rivers's occasional opportunities to alienate himself from his moral and intellectual environment are so productive of insight in the novel.

THE GHOST ROAD

> The First World War goes on getting stronger – our number one national ghost. It's still everywhere, molesting every-body. It's still politically alive, too, in an underground way. On those battlefields the main English social issues surfaced and showed their colours. An English social revolution was fought out in the trenches.
>
> (Hughes, 70)

> Difficult to know what to make of these flashes of cross-cultural recognition. From a professional point of view, they were almost meaningless, but then one didn't have such experiences as a disembodied anthropological intelligence, but as a man, and as a man one had to make some kind of sense of them.
>
> (*The Ghost Road*, 117)

Ted Hughes was writing in 1965, reviewing one of the first anthologies of Great War verse to be issued in the wake of the fiftieth anniversary of the opening of hostilities in 1914. While the immediate cultural legacy of the Second World War was being irreverently challenged, for instance by the Beatle John Lennon's role in Richard Lester's *How I Won the War* (1967), the earlier war was now acquiring the mythic shape and the hold over the contemporary imagination it would sustain over the next half-century.

Barker's reassessment of the national ghost is dependent on that myth-making even as it revises it, and this is why her work yields such interesting reflections on how the war remains 'alive'. The third novel – 'it was always three books' Barker has insisted – is both a conclusion and a geographical commentary on the war's status as secular end times (Brannigan, 2005, 381). It opens wonderfully, with a vignette of wartime Britain at the seaside (Scarborough is where the Manchesters, Owen's regiment, were reforming a battalion in 1918). The scenario nods at the pier and seafront setting of Richard Attenborough's *Oh! What a Lovely War* (1969), the film of the stage work which had, at the beginning of the 1960s, first synthesized and disseminated the central elements of the myth of 'our' Great War. This was the futile war, in which brave men were betrayed by incompetent generals, and it was best rendered not using naturalist devices, but by combining the black humour of soldier's songs and an aesthetics of montage and juxtaposition. Barker's own version of this technique, the creation of an apparently social-realist collage underpinned by a network of lucidly intelligent analogies and correspondences, is rapidly restated: a war-widow reduced to 'tutelage' in her mother's house; Prior about to return to France not out of patriotism or duty but 'fastidiousness'; the revelation that Rivers had 'got his own voice back too'; the rapid adaptation of the language of war – 'over the top' – to civilian sociality (*Ghost*, 6, 13). This pattern of criss-crossing causal and metaphorical relationships acquires a different form – a kind of counterpoint – in the trilogy's concluding volume, a consequence both of bringing the narrative to an end and of the particular materials on which Barker is drawing to create a story of the last days of the war.

The most important of these new materials contributes a Pacific counterpart to the world of the trenches. Prior underestimates the effects of Rivers's recollections of his anthropological field work when he refers to 'a slightly odd perspective on the "present conflict"' (*Ghost*, 215). The impact of the parallels Barker has Rivers recognize is to ask something similar of the reader, but here recognition is not perceiving something as 'the one previously known' or under the familiar category (*OED*), but the acknowledgement of a kinship that modern thinking disowns. The parallels achieve something similar to the observation by the Martiniquan poet and politician Aimé Césaire (1913–2008), that European totalitarianism was a translation of colonial politics back to the Old World (Young, 2).

In *Regeneration* and *The Ghost Road*, Rivers's anthropological imagination has been correlated with theoretical issues in psychoanalysis and neurology, when for instance he speculates, after the manner of a structuralist, about links between the terminology for the way meanings are disguised in dreams (the historical Rivers, 1923, 19, rejected that Freudian thesis), and the interpretation of myth and ritual (*Regeneration*, 186). But in *The Ghost Road* 'cross-cultural connections' mount up from other sources, reflecting the character's continuing interrogation of disciplinary boundaries, and the relationship between the scientist and the human being. Melanesia is first brought to mind by the apparent absurdity of his treatment of Moffet's hysterical paralysis by suggestion: '[a] witch doctor could do this' (*Ghost*, 49). To counterpoint the research on Eddystone with Prior's self-analysis, Barker gives her characters a fever (which restores Rivers's visual memory) and a notebook. Taking Rivers away from England creates an array of similarities which prompt an interrogation of English values. Housekeeper Mrs Irving's 'shrine' to her dead son is 'not fundamentally different from the skull houses of Pa Na Gunda', though it is doubtful Mrs Irving could appreciate this (*Ghost*, 116–17). The 'rows and rows of crosses in the mission graveyard, men and women in the prime of life dead of the diseases of the English nursery' provide a resonant commentary on the funerary architecture of post-war Flanders, particularly the war cemeteries which are a central element in our iconography of the war (*Ghost*, 125). The irony of adults decimated by childhood ailments at once implies racist missionary patronage, and elaborates the generational metaphors which have overlaid the relations of characters in the trilogy. The meanings of priority have been undercut: Prior is worried that he is having flashbacks to bayoneting a 'middle-aged man', when it is proper to mourn 'golden youth', and he has a Pied Piper anxiety about whether they will all come back after the war (Kurt Vonnegut subtitled his anti-war novel *Slaughterhouse-Five* the 'Children's Crusade') (*Ghost*, 218, 241). The anthropologist's methods for establishing kinship would be overwhelmed by these shifting patterns: 'a generation lasted six months . . . . [Prior] was this boy's great-grandfather' (46). The parallel between the ritual clubbing of illegitimates raised as symbolic sons with the sacrifice of Isaac commanded of Abraham is apparently not a parallel at all, but 'the difference between savagery and civilization' (104). But the memory had returned precisely because one of Rivers's sons-by-transference is embarking for France. Another differential is undercut.

The authority vested in the analytic encounter had been challenged long before Prior's resistance, when a Melanesian woman, having answered the kinship questionnaire, insists '[y]our turn':

> their view of *his* society was neither more nor less valid than his of theirs . . . . And with that realization, the whole frame of social and moral rules that keeps individuals imprisoned – and sane – collapsed, and for a moment he was in the same position as these drifting, dispossessed people. A condition of absolute free-fall. (119–20)

The narrative tone here checks academic certitude, the 'whole frame of social and moral rules', with the helter-skelter movements of the mind confronting the paradoxes of experience, 'imprisoned – and sane'. These contraries, thematic and discursive, are emblematic of Barker's achievement in preventing the ideas in her novels from sedimenting into hierarchies, or either/or disjunctions. The ideas are ways of capturing something about a human predicament, but never everything, and never alone.

This fallibility of concepts, and indeed myths, is apparent in the fate of Rivers's efforts to evaluate his therapy, of Prior's 'using myself as a test case'. The thesis is that breakdown is precipitated by passivity rather than 'horrors', and this is the idea which Rivers has extended into a set of speculations about masculinity and femininity (most recently in the case of his sister Kathleen's neurasthenia, which he relates to the Alice-in-Wonderland-like constrictions of her domestic life). But the war is not about being 'cramped in holes' anymore. Now troops are prepared for 'open, mobile warfare ... it's all different', and indeed Owen himself experienced little of what is thought of as the standard Western Front experience (Hibberd, xvii). Significantly, in the last months of the war 'the test's invalid' (*Ghost*, 172). From another perspective, Rivers's successes, the patients that have been returned to active service in France with their nerves steady, are, 'by any civilized standard ... objects of horror' (200).

The other voice in the counterpoint of Eddystone and Flanders is Prior's. From mute to author, the character has developed from a device to irritate Rivers to a device for getting close to Owen in the last days of the war. Indeed, Prior in some senses converges on the historical figure, as if they have literally come to occupy the same space: having avoided each other at Craiglockhart, sharing a billet, and being watched by 'somebody who knows the full terror of the fall' is a disturbingly alienated version of self-scrutiny (148). Prior's journal has an additional splitting effect: 'First-person narrators can't die, so as long as we keep telling the story of our own lives we're safe' (115). The subject of this narrative is another defensive creation, like the fearless, fatherless double born in the shell-hole. This voice is an artistic risk; no longer in agonistic dialogue with its 'betters', the ironies it produces must be consciously articulated, and are in danger of seeming arch.

Having Prior observe Owen from a distance produces a disconcerting effect (note the contrast with the Owen-Sassoon dialogues created from Owen's letters and draft poems):

> I look across at Owen, who's doing casualty reports .... For days after the battle he went round with his tunic stiff with blood, but then I had blood and brains on me. We must have stunk like the drains in a slaughterhouse, but we've long since stopped smelling each other. He looks like one of the boys you see on street corners in the East End. Open to offers. I must say I wouldn't mind. He looks up, feeling himself the subject of scrutiny, smiles and pushes the fags across. I saw him in the attack, caped and masked in blood, seize a machine-gun and turn it on its previous owners at point-blank range. Like killing fish in a bucket. And I wonder if he sees those faces, grey, open-mouthed faces, life draining out of them before the bullets hit, as I see the faces of men I killed in the counter-attack. I won't ask. He wouldn't answer if I did. I wouldn't *dare* ask. For the first time it occurs to me that Rivers's job also requires courage. (199–200)

The mirroring is insistent – both the figures presented in this scene are bloodied, both sexually promiscuous, both liable to the 'return of the repressed', both incommunicative. The acknowledgement of the therapist's courage in trying to breach this silence cannot distract us from the suspicion that the novelist is doing just the same: Prior is the means with which to open up the lives of historical figures beyond their incarnation in the extant archive. But the process is reciprocal, with Prior's inscribed voice incorporating Owen's words: 'My nerves are in perfect working order' (254). The image of Owen is as a consequence transformed – he wrote his mother that 'I only shot one man with my revolver . . . . The rest I took [captured] with a smile' (Owen, *Selected Letters*, 351). Prior's sexual fantasy, together with this substitution of a Macbeth-like warrior, contests Owen's 'sanctity' in a deliberate and somewhat crude way (Heaney, xiv). Barker has discussed the provocation behind her writing of sex:

> Prior has sex with a boy on a canal bank. It's very explicit. Some people are shocked by it. Then a month further on, another group of young men meet on another canal bank, and they kill each other, and I wish I could say the shock was equal. It isn't but perhaps it should be.
>
> (Garland, 196)

Making Owen an 'indifferent' killer is arguably a greater provocation, for it disturbs the national ghost.

The Ghost Road has its share of Barker's ghosts. The author has gone on record about how 'useful' has been her upbringing by spiritualists, in a household where 'the dead were very much part of life' (Brannigan, 388). The war and Melanesia multiply the occasions on which a haunting or some other-worldly entity is invoked to 'make some kind of sense' of experience (*Ghost*, 117). '[M]others looking for contact with lost sons' attend the performances of 'hysterics' (77–8). But if the séance is all too like Craiglockhart for Prior, he can nevertheless employ the language of ghosts in his own characterization of a world at war: 'Ghosts everywhere. Even the living were only ghosts in the making' (46). This is an ironic extrapolation of Sassoon's imagery of 'haunted nights' in his Craiglockhart poem 'Survivors', which vigorously opposes the regeneration of soldiers (Sassoon, 1983, 97). Sassoon's ghosts disappear when he negates the warning of this poem by returning to France:

> The ghosts were not an attempt at evasion, Rivers thought, either by Sassoon or by the islanders. Rather, the questions became more insistent, more powerful, for being projected into the mouths of the dead. (212)

This last rationalization admits its own limits with that acknowledgement of the power of haunting speech, which becomes one of the novel's symbols for the inexpressible. Rivers on Eddystone struggles with a 'language barrier', exacerbated by the existence of a tongue he was not permitted to hear, 'the language of ghosts'. He translates his native informant referring to ghosts as 'a figure of speech' (164), an expedience which makes the question an anthropological, not a metaphysical one. On Eddystone 'no division really made sense' and 'ghosts and sex *did* go together'; that is, these cultural themes don't carve up in ways a European would anticipate (133). But Europeans' experience no longer responds so docilely to enumeration within the old categories. Sex and war have a striking proximity in the novel. Prior imagines it will take a 100 years of war for 'another language to evolve, one that was capable of describing the sound of a bombardment' because '[t]here are no words' available to him to say what battle sounds like, or to describe his visual hallucination of the sun rising at dusk (198).

Sharon Ouditt has posed the question whether the writing of fiction about the Great War at the end of the twentieth century indicates some 'return of the culture's repressed horrors' (Sherry, 257). But we might wonder whether our appetite for representations of war experience, manifest everywhere from the cinema to the A level syllabus, has other meanings. We appear to require that what is repressed by participants in war be made manifest throughout civil society (a definition of modern war literature is that it is realist rather than idealist, it describes war 'as it is', not as heroic codes imply it ought to be). Culturally successful representations of war (those which are widely reproduced) can be thought of as integrating war into a larger scheme of values, but of course this achievement involves other modes of repression and censorship.

Artists representing war may seek other goals than integrative comprehension, and thereby draw our attention to the consequences of the rationalizations with which violence is made sense of. Barker's emphasis on discordant themes and values, and her development of forms which multiply rather than harmonize perspectives, place her firmly in the party which promotes the reader's apprehension of contradiction. But it is striking that this has not been an obstacle to the dissemination of her writing about the Great War, which not only made her name but which relatively swiftly acquired cultural status as literature to be studied alongside the canonical writing about 1914–18 on the AQA A level syllabus. The cynical might point to a writer cashing in on a subject, which, as the novelist Michèle Roberts put it, is 'bigger and brighter than the conventional feminine sphere' (quoted in Monteith, 2005, 106). Sebastian Faulks and Louis de Bernières are among contemporaries who have turned research into 'little-known' corners of World Wars into literary bestsellers, but this is not an explanation of the reception of such representations. The incorporation of the trilogy into an extended canon of Great War writing is a symptom of what Barker herself diagnoses, that the war is far from over (see *Another World*). If shellshock is 'still one of the most powerful imaginative symbols of the Great War' this is because the term meshes the physical and the mental, world and representation, in a complex of values which cannot, yet, be reduced to a singular account (Micale and Lerner, 207). It is Barker's achievement to incarnate the dynamic of this symbolic and mythic afterlife of the Great War in the form of her novels. Moreover, she regenerates that afterlife by meshing it with a reflexive, retrospective revaluation of the historical discourses which have formed it.

5

ANOTHER WORLD AND *BORDER CROSSING*

ANOTHER WORLD

> We speak so much of memory because there is so little of
> it left.
>
> (Nora, 7)

Another World presents a contemporary England full of dangers –
that is certainly how its inhabitants perceive it – and the novel
counterpoints these threats with revenants of the Great War. Nick,
an academic psychologist, lives in the 'shadow of monstrosities':
Peter Sutcliffe, Fred and Rose West and the children who murdered James Bulger are specifically alluded to as the ubiquitous,
mediated images of the violence of the age (*Another World*, 3).
Nick is threatened – by the youths in Newcastle's Bigg Market, by
his daughter's pubescence – but he has also learned threatening
behaviour, edging his car at the legs of lads scuffling across the
road and gesturing offensively at other motorists (later in the story
he is convinced he has run over a girl, as if the aggressiveness of his
motoring makes this a likely outcome). The modern everyday is a
war zone. Urban dereliction fills the windscreen and serves as an

injunction to keep moving – like a war correspondent's footage on TV; Summerfield, with the old Fanshawe armaments factory boarded-up, is 'Beirut-on-Tyne' (11).

Another World involves a restaging and re-examination of some of the leading themes of the trilogy – war, masculinity, memory, therapy, generations and ghosts – in the context of late twentieth-century social and family dysfunction. It also puts the historical imagination into dialogue with rival conceptions of the past. The North-East of the early novels is now seen from the perspective of a proprietor's residence, rather like the Wynyard's home in *Liza's England*. Not only has Barker's dominant point of view shifted from a female to a male one, so has the perspective become 'middle-class, Hampstead-style', professional and risk-conscious, that is materially affluent but spiritually precarious (137).

Another World, however, is as much a recession or withdrawal from the trilogy and its historical reference as a repetition, and Barker is prepared to cast an ironical gaze over some of the motifs and devices which were responsible for its great success. The tone of the novel is another departure. A ghost story with comic allusions to *Wuthering Heights*, it is at the same time an essay on memory and a dramatic study of adolescence and dying, of parenting and being a child. It also contains some authoritative writing about the banality of violence and loss. Apparitions and unbidden returns link the novel to the four narratives preceding it, but most closely to *The Man Who Wasn't There*, whose form also balances the comic and the portentous.

The novel very subtly deploys proportion, and in particular the ratio of concern for one's own world and indifference to others' worlds, which is a consequence of the egocentrism which divides even families and lovers. So, for Nick's new wife, the pregnant Fran, shopping with children is a 'nightmare', exacerbated by the fact that her partner is off caring for a dying grandfather: '[i]t's the sort of thing you'd like to blot out of your consciousness for ever' (135). This is the text-book explanation of trauma, but the definition of these mental states is already leaking away in metaphor. They are however concretely instanced in the life of the old man, Geordie, who is in another world, 'a world of his own', 'no man's land', experiencing a return of the past in horrific dreams or nightmares, a return which has the force to displace the reality of the present (70, 168). The ways in which these experiences, and their representation (in this instance, maternal stress and post-traumatic stress disorder (PTSD)), both overlap and yet do not connect is enriched by the presence of a further other world. This is suggested by the gothic revenants associated with the story of the Fanshawe family, introduced by the device of the return of the hate-filled family cartoon 'repressed' beneath the wallpaper. Wallpaper was Prior's favourite taunt at Rivers's therapeutic detachment (*Regeneration*, 51, 106). Here it symbolizes a mode of survival predicated on not being too perspicacious: 'It's us', insists Nick's daughter Miranda, registering how the cartoon seems to depict the tensions in her own modern, temporarily reassembled family, but both Fran and Nick are determined to bypass this recognition.

The formal dimension of this interest in proportion is well-illustrated by the thirteenth chapter, which performs a sequence of steps backward or recessions designed to undercut cultural norms concerning children and violence (William Golding did something similar, although using a different technique, in *The Lord of the Flies* (1954), to which Barker's stone-throwing episode alludes). This chapter opens with a neat tripling, worked around the motif of the face at the window (recalling the acme of literary ghost stories, Henry James's *The Turn of the Screw* (1898)): Miranda sees the figure of a girl at the window (she fears it is the infanticidal Fanshawe daughter), baby Jasper is terrified by Miranda's inquisitive re-enactment of the 'haunting', Gareth is terrified that the girls from the Summerfield estate are stalking him. The chapter will resolve on a different sequencing, with Jasper unable to see Gareth on the cliff, and Gareth convinced he's been watched by Miranda. These threats/punishments are one way of thinking about what frightens children, but they also underpin the presentation of the fearful things children are capable of doing. It isn't that Gareth doesn't know right from wrong; he's just struggling to negotiate a world full of confusing signals: the baby 'never gets wrong for anything', mum says 'I'll bloody murder you,' and he is being killed and getting back-up all the time in his role-play computer games. Fear and frustration are the forces shaping Gareth's world. He fears Nick's size, and the kids at the big secondary school he'll be attending next term; smaller things are available for expressing hurt through hurting. In this respect the rock pools on the beach are a theatre of violence because they are already a scaled-down world, like Gareth's toy sniper:

> You squat down and look into the pool and it's a bit like *Jurassic Park* – you're like a dinosaur looking through a car window at the helpless squealing wriggling pink kids inside. (183)

Jasper, seen from the cliff top, is 'small and pink'; Gareth is sticking within the rules of a game because he is aiming to miss (188). The proximity of play to violence is brilliantly captured in this episode, which depathologizes the instincts of Wansbeck in *The Ghost Road*, who is afraid of being left alone with people lest he kill them. Gareth is so frightened of having crossed a boundary by opening Jasper's head with a rock that he has to go on; he must stop the crying, and the discovery crying will inevitably bring. This motif of the slippage from play to murder is revisited in the childhoods of Tom and Danny, psychologist and murderer, in *Border Crossing*. It is an emblem of that we are uneasy at acknowledging as part of ourselves, of regions of experience which in the twentieth-century have been pathologized (another Foucauldian exclusion) but which Barker seems intent on bringing back into contact with the ordinary.

In *Another World*, Gareth's bullying has two analogues: the story of the Fanshawe infanticide, and Geordie's closely guarded memory, the mercy killing of his fatally wounded brother which, under the deforming pressures of maternal preference, the culture of remembrance and involuntary flashbacks arcing across 80 years, he now believes to have been fratricide. Not only does the novel resonate with the 'horrific' unnaturalness of these events, and with the way they confound legal and ethical norms – 'the Fanshawe children had got away with murder,' the message of war is *'You can get away with it'* (112, 85) – it seeks to understand all these valuations in the context of regimes of representation.

For while Geordie has been caught up again in his past, literally so in the present-tense flashbacks which diagnose PTSD, he also has a prominent social function as a vehicle of memory in a contemporary culture of remembrance. This celebrity is the subject of a flirtatious contest between two professionals, his grandson Nick, a Psychology professor who is 'fantastic with other people's problem kids', and Helen, an academic historian alert to the malleability of traces of the past. Their debate is a reframing of issues which arise from Barker's writing of the trilogy, in particular questions about the purpose and the ethics of recreating of the past.

The return of Geordie's nightmares, the 'baggage' he'd brought back from France, is mirrored by an anxiety over the last veterans of the war (63). Soon there will be no more men who served in the war to take part in remembrance parades and to tell us how it really was (the idea of the last veteran periodically resurfaced in the serious press after the Millennium). It is as if the possibility of testimonial recall represents an unmedited connection with the past (hence the strategic importance of testimony in the construction of a non-Nazi archive of the Holocaust, such as Steven Spielberg's video testimony project). The use of interviews with combatant veterans had been an innovation in the now legendary BBC 26-part series *The Great War* (1964), written by historians John Terraine and Corelli Barnett, a series which helped invent television history. But testimony is not neutral; it is, like the output of the psychoanalytic encounter, shaped by transference and counter-transference. And as the historian Dan Todman has suggested, when the Great War generation began to die out, their testimony became part of the national mythology, and an object of nostalgia (Todman, 197).

There is a sense in which Helen's assembling of veterans' memories for her oral history book *Soldier, from the Wars Returning* is a latter-day version of spiritualism, a summoning of voices to speak from what, in this case, will very shortly be a realm beyond personal remembrance. Ironically Geordie's testimony is found wanting first by his spiritualist mother, who 'remembered the dead so [she] could forget the living with a clear conscience' (155), then by the suspicious thesis of Helen's book. She is convinced that such autobiographical memories are fallible; soldiers 'remake' their memories to 'fit in with public perceptions of the war' (83). This idea has been explored by the oral historian Alistair Thomson, whose 1994 study, *ANZAC Memories: Living with the Legend*, considered the impact of cinema among other factors in the shaping and convergence of veteran's recollections. In a decade in which '[m]emory [was] decidedly in fashion', in both the 'retrieval of neglected memories' and as a 'bulwark of identity politics', this was just another class of false memory (Wood, 1).

Barker bridges the distance between war and these contemporary theories of memory as a social construct, by reinstating the therapeutic scenario of *Regeneration*. The persistence of nightmares calls forth models of therapy whose very promise of regeneration or restitution is a travesty of the predicament of the sufferer. Helen's and Nick's relationships with the old man are overlaid by a detached, even bureaucratic professional concern, as is signalled by her interest in the way he has 'manage[d] his memories' (241). This contrasts with the embodied care of Geordie's wife, recorded in his taped rendition of her nightmare-lullaby, 'Keep your feet still . . . And dinnet drive me bonny dreams away': being in the same bed as the sick is a powerful, recurring image of family in Barker's work, and Nick never gets this close, even to Helen (258).

Nick and Helen have become rivals for an abstract guardianship of Geordie's memories, with their competing theories, the one scientific and biological, the other anti-foundational and sociological. And of course Geordie has his own views about the memory of war and the responsibilities of the survivors, and this includes haunting the tidily reconstructed trench in the Imperial War Museum and telling young visitors that back then 'you were frightened and wanted to go home.' Geordie is a one-man warning-from-history: '*It happened once, therefore it can happen again. Take care*' (84, 82). In this connection he wants to recruit his grandson as a kind of memory relay. Their trip to the battlefields of the Somme – a form of memorial tourism initiated in the years immediately after the war, and the subject of Adam Thorpe's novel *Nineteen Twenty-One* (2001) – is Geordie's attempt 'to graft his memories on to Nick' (74). The effect of the pilgrimage to the vast 1932 Monument to the Missing of the Somme at Thiepval is ultimately to overcome Nick's resistance to the architecture and the rituals of remembrance: for him the 'annihilating abstractions' of Edwin Lutyen's arch had 'represented not a triumph *over* death, but the triumph of death' (72–4). Nick is actually rather sceptical about annihilating the past by revisiting it, and about the answer to present problems being locatable in prior experience: 'You think if he tells you everything it'll wipe out the past,' he lectures Fran after Gareth has injured Jasper: ' "It's good to talk," ' he adds mockingly, quoting a 1980s advertising strap for the privatized British Telecom (205). The commodification of conversation and the promise of a therapeutic culture cannot be told apart:

as the sociologist Frank Furedi has suggested, 'the system of therapy is not confined to a distinct and functionally specific role, it has merged with wider cultural institutions' (Furedi, 17).

Nick has no room in his worldview for the concept of 'public memory', a term (alongside popular memory and collective memory) which has been in increasing circulation since the 1990s. Public memory designates a sense of the past which is neither first-personal recall, nor history; it is more immediately bound up with the processes through which a culture reproduces itself than is the past represented in the archives of historiography or by official sites of memory such as Thiepval. Nick objects to the concept on the grounds that memory is just 'a biochemical change in an individual brain': it is an autobiographical trace, not a shared or indeed aspirational meaning in perpetual renegotiation. His best evidence in this argument is traumatic memory: the involuntary character of recall convinces him such memories are 'not accessible to language . . . it's like acting in a film' (85)

But Helen's case that the past is not persistent, but mutable, is also made a persuasive one in the novel. She believes she has evidence that Geordie's willingness to talk about his war experience is proportional to the amount of talk about the war going on in the culture at large. If he once had to repress negative memories of war because they were culturally unacceptable, the 1960s changed everything:

> A later generation, fresh from a visit to *Oh! What a Lovely War* (sic), the *Dies Irae* of Britten's *War Requiem* pounding in its ears, couldn't get enough of fear, pain, etc. The horror, the horror. Give us more. Suddenly a large part of Geordie's experience was 'acceptable', though still not all. (83)

This social, as opposed to psychotherapeutic, model of the integration of traumatic experience might imply that the veteran can now achieve some kind of equilibrium, his own past in phase with public history (recall the importance for war literature of the figure of an epistemological division between Western Front and Home Front). But the glancing allusion to Conrad – Kurtz's dying words ('The horror! The horror!') turned into a consumerist slogan – contains the counter-suggestion that acceptance is morbid and perverse as much as it is a wakening to historical reality.

Cultural 'progress' – in Fussell's argument the emergence of emblems adequate to historical adversity – appears to be a variant of the healing effects of time, or of therapy's aspiration to shift tenses for the patient, so that 'I am in hell' is transformed into something he has passed.

Nick's mourning for his grandfather begins with an angry refusal of the hymnal's 'Time, like an ever rolling stream,' with its balm of forgetting:

> It's too easy to dismiss somebody else's lived experience as a symptom of this, that, or the other pathology: to label it, disinfect it, store it away neatly in slim buff files and prevent it making dangerous contact with the experience of normal people. But suppose . . . you're wrong and he was right. Suppose it's not an ever rolling stream, but something altogether more viscous and unpredictable, like blood. Suppose it coagulates around terrible events, clots over them, stops the flow. Suppose Geordie experienced time differently, because, for him, time was different? It's nonsense, of course. And just as well, because if true, it would be far more terrible than anything the passage of time can deliver. Recovery, rehabilitation, regeneration, redemption, resurrection, remembrance itself, all meaningless, because they all depend on that constantly flowing stream. (271)

In its self-defensive acceptance of the healing effects of time, the passage appears to enact mourning in the Freudian sense of a detachment from the lost object of love, but it also reminds us of the work that must go into sustaining identities. The image of the bloodstream gives resonance to the pathology of the everyday, which is characterized here as a form of quarantine which conserves the 'normal', a category which the novel does everything possible to negate. The hydraulic image of time perhaps reminds us too of Graham Swift's handling of the memory of historical and private disaster in *Waterland* (1983), a novel of the amphibious fens, of metaphors of flows and blockages, floods and sediments, as well as of disjunctions between historiographical and personal narratives of the past. Stories are 'a way of bearing what won't go away', academic history a reminder of 'mistakes' (Swift, 194, 203). But the difference in the status of the historical in the two novels is very striking (and should warn us about too swiftly deciding on the trends in historical consciousness in our own times). In *Waterland*, the narrator is a history teacher who presides over the end of history (the subject has been axed from the syllabus by labour market *diktat*); in *Another World* there is no end of history: history is in the market and doing very well for itself.

The way in which Barker represents the works of the characters in *Another World* who are historical writers invites us to speculate on how the author's mode of historical fiction, to which she returns in *Life Class* (2007), is related to the sense of the past promulgated in popular culture and public life. Veronica Laidlaw is a 'prolific historical novelist' who reveals an 'interest in crime' with her *Mary Ann Cotton's Teapot and Other Notable Northern Murders*. The work is 'anything but sensational', despite the way it has been marketed as heritage gothic (106–7). The extract which Nick reads reveals how lame is this judgement, and Barker takes the opportunity to weave further ironies into the texture of the novel. Jeremiah Cookson, the discredited witness in the case, bears the name of the perennially popular South Shields writer of historical romances, Catherine Cookson (1906–98) 'who when she was ten years old tried to drown another child', and who is thus an example, Barker has suggested in interview, of bullying which was not pushed to a 'tragic outcome' (Stevenson, 180). Cookson's evidence is dismissed because he had a 'canny few' to drink, a nice joke against a text dependent for its effects on an overblown evocation of the uncanny, notably the reported sighting of the children with the Guy: 'the creaking trolley, with its grotesquely masked burden, haunted the imagination. People had nightmares about it' (110). There is something cartoon-like about the image of Robert Fanshawe's body 'impaled on the uncut German wire surrounded by unexploded British shells', a too-deliberate juxtaposition which reduces the industrial and generational themes of *The Eye in the Door* to the bathetic 'bad luck' (112).

Laidlaw's invocation of 'public opinion' is the clue to the designs her narrative has on the contemporary reader; revulsion and fascination, bafflement and summary judgement constitute a thread of supposed common sense ('[t]he horror, the horror. Give us more') linking those who followed the trial with those who delight in its resurrection as an informative and entertaining episode of local history, part of the texture of a communal life which survives only as an effect of the heritage economy. Helen has a wholly different interest in 'public perceptions' (83), which she views as normative pressures on what individuals can recognize, or accept, as their own apprehensions and their own memories. But as a revisionist historian, one determined to alter the dominant interpretation of the past, she cannot help anticipating the 'correct' line of development of public knowledge, which should trail after the academic vanguard. We see this in her demonstration to Geordie that a residue of his experience remains unpalatable to the public appetite for the past:

> he still hadn't been asked to talk about class, the different experiences of officers and men, profiteering, the whole idea of the war as a business in which some people suffered and died to make others rich, though this bitterness, as much as the anguish of grief for lost comrades, had shaped and framed his experience of the post-war years. (83)

This is to equate Geordie's acceptable memories with a collective amnesia, a burying of the discordant or dissident elements in the national past.

These made-up historical renderings of past violence invite us to scrutinize Barker's own brand of writing with, about and against history. However, to assume that Helen's critical historiography is the superior discourse would be to miss the meanings which the novel disseminates. Helen's efforts to modernize the testimony she works with read like a travesty of the procedures of the trilogy, in particular the issue of its imaginative anachronism: '[s]he tried to get Geordie to frame his war experience in terms of late-twentieth-century preoccupations. Gender. Definitions of masculinity. Homoeroticism' (83). Of course, critics who observe that Barker's presentation of the Great War is at variance with the true status of psychoanalysis within the British medical establishment, or involves an 'anachronistic' handling of the words of the war poets, need to remember that novels are invested with historiographical authority by readers, reviewers and teachers, as well as by their authors: the TV historian Ben Shepherd has overlooked this, the academic critic Fran Brearton acknowledges it (Shepherd, 2000, 109; Brearton, 2007, 209). Geordie's 'Homo-*what?*' confounds the broad sweep of 'construction of the past' arguments, pitching the old man's rejection of categories that mean nothing to him against the social historian's awareness that the meanings we live by are perennially renewed. The past cannot be an entirely 'foreign country' (as L. P. Hartley's narrator in *The Go-Between*, 1953, insists) so long as it is in any kind of dialogue with the present, and Geordie of course is as keen to maintain this dialogue as anyone.

If *Notable Northern Murderers* supplies more of the 'same old thing', *Soldier, from the Wars Returning* is intended to radicalize the past. But it remains a function of what Martin Davies has called 'an already historicized world' in which 'experience cannot be conceived *except* in the shape of past events', like Geordie's warning (Davies, 3). Helen's researches and reasoning are parodied in the 'historical' investigations of *Border Crossing*, where Danny's professed interest in finding out what happened is a cover for a manipulative and systematic revision of the version of events that has stood until now.

Penelope Lively's Booker prize-winning novel *Moon Tiger* (1987) explores the idea of history through the death-bed meditations of its historian narrator Claudia, who reflects not only on the past, but also on the forms of its survival. Her faith is lodged in the composite voice of history, the idea that history is argument, disagreement and contention, 'my word against yours; this evidence against that' (Lively, 14). One ex-lover is a methodological rival, a 'television mogul' whose expensive and meticulous reconstructions of the Second World War diminish the past as they cut it into slots for the entertainment-craving audiences of the newly dominant medium. The voice of another lover, killed in the fighting in the North African desert in the early 1940s, is restored in the form of a lost journal (Lively's restoration of this voice draws evocatively on the desert war writing of poet Keith Douglas). But if the past depends on the relay of words, it is arguably imaginative fiction which is most enduring: 'Pierre on the field of battle . . . nailed down for ever, on the page and in a million heads' (Lively, 6). But a further irony is set in motion by Lively's choice of the acme of historical fiction, Tolstoy's *War and Peace* (1865–69), as Claudia's example, an irony which confirms the obdurateness of the fictive in an entirely different sense. For Tolstoy failed to nail down Prince Andrey, who was supposed to die at the battle of Austerlitz (1805) in an earlier version, but who was resurrected by the logic of the emerging form of the greatest novel of history, and of the fog of war. *Another World* is not about nailing things down either. The historical and therapeutic conundrums it raises to consciousness are obdurately unresolved beyond the narrative's apparently happy ending.

BORDER CROSSING

The core issues invoked by *Border Crossing* – how our culture represents and negotiates brutality, the nature of personal identity and the question whether or not a person can change – are framed by the themes which dominated Barker's fiction in the 1990s: violence, memory and therapy. This is a novel about crime but, rather surprisingly, given Barker's readiness to confront and shock the reader, the crime remains veiled, even as the implied revelation of horrors serves as an engine of suspenseful momentum. However, the transgressions indicated by the title are not only those associated with criminality or with deviance, but are also those perpetrated by a therapist who is out-of-bounds. When deviations from norms of conduct are pathologized – Tom Seymour's specialism in psychology is 'conduct disorder' – they bring into being new sets of boundaries. And new risks and opportunities flow from the permeability of these boundaries (170). *Border Crossing* represents a development of Barker's interest in the emergent rules of therapy, a theme introduced through the charismatically interdisciplinary figure of W. H. R. Rivers, and the way his relationships with Sassoon and Prior interrupted the ideal type of the analytic encounter.

The novel's subject – the rehabilitation of a child killer – is a potentially incendiary one, as is suggested by the press hue and cry at the novel's climax, which threatens to compromise the expensive, state-sponsored identity of 'Ian Wilkinson'. This frenzied unearthing of a carefully buried past, for the sake of the headlines used to stoke public indignation over *another* murder of an old woman by 'little boys', is in contrast to the charged but ambivalent process of recovering the past which is acted out between Dr Seymour and Danny (164). 'I can be Danny with you' is a Manichaean identification, implying both the search for a lost past and the persistence of the past which has apparently been left behind: the unrecognized Danny '*had* changed' (76, 19). The narrative, in common with the author's previous half-dozen novels, is not only a relating of experience, but takes the form of a self-conscious inquiry into the way that the past can be known and constituted. In this respect, the therapeutic dialogue is as central, formally as well as thematically, as it was in *Regeneration*. Indeed, echoes of the trilogy are important counter-weights to the manipulation and fantasy which distort the sessions in *Border Crossing*, sessions which lack formalized boundaries and in which roles are confused.

Danny is a successor to Billy Prior, not just to Prior the antagonistic and flirtatious patient but to the dissociated Prior, whose 'double' is formed, in a parody of *Genesis*, from the clay of Flanders. This is just how Danny emerges, as yet unrecognized by Tom, who has pulled him from the river: 'Black and glistening, [Danny] lay there, a creature formed, apparently, of mud' (5). The mud doesn't only function to defer Tom's remembering Danny. That *Border Crossing*'s opening involves a memory of an earlier text might alert us to the play of memory more generally, and the question of the relations of what is remembered to what occurred. There is a false memory at the very beginning, and it is Tom's: 'when he looked back on that day, he remembered what he couldn't possibly have seen: a gull's eye view' (2). This instance of memory's fallibility points towards the problems implicit in the project of return or recovery to which the novel's protagonists dedicate themselves. That project is justified by Danny's claim to want to 'work out why it happened', find out why it was that he has a murderous past from which even the most idealistic interventions of state agents of rehabilitation cannot disconnect him (57).

But if the novel's therapeutic sessions are bound up with laying bare the narrative of Danny's life, they are also being used in an attempt to recompose that narrative. He sets out systematically to convince Tom that his evaluation of the child in the case was wrong. The faultiness of Tom's recollection in the opening pages anticipates the way his memories of the case will be shown to be awry, marking out, too, the beginning of this re-authored case-study of Danny as suspect. Additionally, in making sense of their 'extraordinary' reunion, the characters all act as though a human design or pretence were less plausible or portentous an explanation than the concept of coincidence. In the work of writers like Iain Sinclair and W. G. Sebald, or the film-maker Patrick Keiller, coincidence is the form in which meaning arises from the nonsensical, and simultaneously a symptom of desire for overarching or underpinning systems of knowledge. In *Border Crossing*,

a conceptual version of Gresham's law seems to be in operation –
bad ideas drive out good – whereby belief in a metaphysics implied
by coincidence is called forth in proportion to its straining of cred-
ibility (61). 'No point saying you don't believe in coincidences,'
thinks Danny's social worker, Martha, as she struggles to adjust
reality to fit with her convictions (70). Coincidence 'makes you
think', but thinking can be the problem. Tom, with his faith in reason, cannot recognize this as he reasons away the possibility that
Danny has sought him out: '[i]t made no sense' (16–17). Danny
appears to perform the greatest leap of faith, but because his moti-
vations are so obscure, it is only later that we learn to distrust such
moves as naked manipulations of the vulnerable therapist:

> 'I know you're going to laugh, but I still think that wasn't an accident.'
> You and me both, Tom thought. 'So what was it, then?'
>   'It was, I dunno, a sort of kick in the pants, I suppose, because I'd
> tried to go on ignoring it and pretending it didn't happen and suddenly
> there it is, bang. Right in front of me.' (56)

What is right in front of him is the reprise of a therapeutic relationship. But the repetition is presented as returning in order to move
on. Tom is the reason Danny hasn't had any treatment: '[y]ou were
the one who told the court I was normal' (57). His defence –
that he had diagnosed Danny with a pathology, 'post traumatic
stress disorder' – only reinforces Danny's apparently strong hand
in this wager, namely that his rehabilitation has really been uninterrupted repression, leaving the big problem untouched. In presenting himself as someone with a past to be exhumed, Danny is
playing up to the therapist in Tom: it isn't so much the coincidence
on the river that should alarm him, as the coincidence of Danny's
needs and his professional ideology. In a neat inversion of the
iatrogenic pathology (one brought into existence by the medical
profession), here we have a pathology invented by the patient as
a kind of snare. But this isn't attention-seeking Munchausen syndrome; it is something more sinister, and it explodes the categories
of doctor and patient.

The opening scene, in which Tom apparently rescues Danny
from suicidal drowning, is a reworking of the celebrated
ballooning-accident overture to Ian McEwan's *Enduring Love*
(1997), whose narrator also has an Audenesque vision, as 'through

the eyes of the buzzard we had watched earlier' (McEwan, 1). Barker has subsequently cited this fiction, with its characters who 'run towards a catastrophe', as an example of 'dilemma at the heart of writing' (Monteith, 2004, 34), the creation of the undecidable which sustains the writing of the novel. McEwan's narrator actually describes himself 'racing into this story and its labyrinths', which fits Tom's predicament very well: having dived in and then surrendered to Danny's plot, he only belatedly apprehends the problems with which repeating an earlier professional relationship with the boy will confront his integrity as a practitioner (McEwan, 1). The echo of McEwan's stalker-narrative – which trailed a putative 'source' in the form of a case study from the bogus *British Review of Psychiatry* – yields a further significance when we recognize how Barker has routed the contagion of delusion which underpins the vertiginous effects of *Enduring Love* into the therapeutic relation itself. Where McEwan presents the erosion of the science writer's authority, Barker dramatizes the idealism and vulnerability of the therapist who is seduced by his patient.

Pat Barker has argued that the therapeutic setting in *Border Crossing* has an essentially different function to that of the *Regeneration* trilogy: Dr Seymour and 'Ian Wilkinson' 'behave[e] like historians ... rather than like psychologist and patient' (Garland, 196). This is illuminating, but it also elides the significance of the repetition of Prior's antagonism towards Rivers in the mimicry with which Danny accomplishes strategic reversals of therapeutic roles. If the talk between the two men does correspond to Penelope Lively's 'composite' voice of history, 'my word against yours', this is also the undermining of the ambition of therapy. Danny's and Tom's abuse of therapy's core relationship has the effect of introducing a historical determinism which comes close to Geordie's conviction that it could all happen again (just one of the stories about himself with which Danny attempts to displace Tom's earlier professional judgements).

Read as a narrative of historical enquiry, *Border Crossing* is a therapeutic encounter without the promise of healing, the form of the analysis without the meaning. Danny wants to know what happened – contemporaneously he believed he hadn't murdered Lizzie because he had 'believed his own story' – and now he doesn't 'want therapy', doesn't want to 'feel better', he just wants to 'know why' (73, 58). Tom, he claims, 'want[s] it to be doctor and patient' but this is just another instance of the camouflage with which Danny disguises his motives (58). But Tom is, accidentally, predisposed to recognize Danny as a historical case. He is in the middle of writing a study of 'moral thinking in children with conduct disorder', illustrated with case histories 'fictionalized' to protect the identities of former patients (22–3). The return of Danny as the object of 'Ian Wilkinson's' enquiries is a rare chance to 'follow up a case', rather than simply transcribe and summarize it (82). In *The Ghost Road*, Barker presents Rivers's reflexive approach to therapy through Prior's 'experimental' return to combat. Here was a chance to test a speculative form of treatment, a test which was at the same time a confrontation with the therapist's doubts about his role in the continuation of war.

Tom Seymour shares some of Rivers's flexibility of mind – therapy-sceptics, like the creative writing instructor Angus MacDonald, recognize that he doesn't repeat or parrot professional rhetoric – but the difference between the two men is really brought out by the way Barker presents their interaction with their patients. Prior, who had been created as a provocation to the Rivers character, presses him to confront his own past. This involves untangling the history of Rivers's own neurotic symptoms and their relation to Victorian codes of warrior masculinity. Tom Seymour's past is similarly opened up by Danny's usurpation of the therapist's role in the analytic exchange, but in a more dangerous way, for while Tom reflects on his childhood as a result of re-examining his other cases, his sessions with Danny bring his professional competence into doubt. The measure of Rivers's prowess in Barker's fiction is his openness to paradox, including the contradictions in his own conduct and beliefs. Tom, by contrast, is never granted the perspective which is credited to Rivers (tacitly, through his focalization of the trilogy's major themes): here it is the doubling or paired orbiting of Tom and Danny in session which is the engine of analogical insight.

Historical research into Daniel Miller is a narrative means of simultaneously bringing the therapeutic profession into doubt, and emplotting revenge on the practitioner – Tom in his earlier role as expert witness – who helped determine which consequences were visited on the murderous boy. Going over the past brings into play a range of concepts – memory and story, causality and responsibility, justice and redemption – which cumulatively have the effect of undermining Tom and of further destabilizing contemporary representations of violence and of masculinity.

'Ian hasn't got any memories,' that is he represents the empty promise of those agencies which supervised Danny's getting past what he did as a boy (70). At Long Garth 'the past didn't matter' (177). Thus oblivion is at the root of the secure unit's now unfashionable ideology of rehabilitation. Boys are abetted in forgetting by an institutional repression of the past. In the words, themselves an over-rehearsed self-quotation, of its headmaster Bernard Greene, 'this is the first day of the rest of your life. I don't care what you've done . . . . The moment you walk through that gate you start living forwards' (123). Tom is slow to pick up on the contradictions in Danny's proposition that coincidence opens the way to remedy this neglect of the child's need for treatment, rather than containment. Specifically, his disavowal of healing is at odds with his demonstration that Tom's expertise produced the subject who was first convicted and incarcerated. Danny's doubly repressed memories of what he did to the body of Lizzie become at this point the putative object of a historical inquiry. But the narrative's real interest lies not in a historical act of violence but in the possibility of further violence which its protagonists respectively overlook and disguise.

Tom, by contrast, does have memories, and these are introduced in the interstices of work and a private life which consists in mid-life upheaval and loss, as he pays a visit to his widowed mother. He is still mourning his father 2 years on; the widow's single, unvisited existence is an admonitory image of his own prospects, particularly the absence of 'white heat of bodily closeness', as his wife exits their childless marriage (43). The infertility of this relationship seems to stand more generally for the absence of development, for the daunting influence of the doctor father and the risk of 'total selfishness, that dreadful, terminal boyishness of men who can't stop thinking of themselves as young' because they haven't lived inside the paternal role (26). Barker's handling of childhood and fatherhood in this novel might constructively be compared with the poet Blake Morrison's prose meditations on being the son of a doctor (who like Tom's dad lacks the patience which he urges upon his patients), and on the meaning of the child and of childhood in the wake of the James Bulger case, respectively *And When Did You Last See Your Father?* (1993) and *As If* (1998).

The narrative insists that it isn't just reminders of the lost contentedness of childhood that lead Tom to make a literal return to
a place he once played in, but that Danny Miller had been at the
back of his mind. The memory evoked involves a detailed repetition of Gareth's baby-battering violence from *Another World*, but in
the new fictional context, and in contrast with Danny's violence,
the scene issues in an even more chilling sense of the contingency
of moral disaster. Tom's part in bombarding a little boy stuck in
a pond is described as an instinctual solution to the threat that
'they were going to get into trouble'; the destructive escalation of
force represents a blind hope that the situation will go away. Only
the miraculous intervention of a witness on a bus meant 'three
children were saved that day' (48). The reversal of the abduction
of James Bulger (three childhoods ended, the witnesses who did
nothing) underlines Tom's good fortune compared with Danny,
for whom there was no timely adult supervision. This differential resurfaces in Tom's guilt over his complicity in the social
oblivion of the Price family and their council estate environment.
Danny's misfortune it to have assaulted a moral geography as well
as old lady, a symbol as well as a person; murder by a child in
rural England means something different to the same behaviour
on the estate (116). But Tom seems to miss the significance of
the other connection which he recognizes in this uncanny shared
past. What interests him about his memories of the incident which
could have destroyed three lives is that 'the sense of moral responsibility was missing.' There is an aporia in his life story: 'In spite
of the connecting thread of memory, the person who'd done
that was not sufficiently like his present self for him to feel guilt'
(48). Indeed, the repeated motif of the child-offender's 'hot face'
pressed against the psychologist's body insinuates a tug of sympathetic identification that is absent from his recollections of self.
Thus, and despite his own detachment, Tom is prepared to go
along with Danny's putative quest for the missing link, the memory which will complete the explanatory life story into a unity.
In part this willingness reflects Tom's excess of hope over experience, his desire to help even where he is sceptical about the
benefits his therapeutic techniques can bring. But this unwariness
is also a figure for unarticulated threat of Danny, a young man
who has made a career out of flattering other people's sense of
vocation.

Tom will ultimately see that Danny's 'rambling excursions into the past' have been designed as 'a systematic rebuttal of the evidence' he had given in court (191). The fallibility of Tom's memory again serves to blind him to Danny's motives, for, as the defense solicitor corrects him, Tom's evidence ensured that what the jury at the trial had in mind was 'not a nice little boy, but a precocious little killer' (85). Danny's hostility towards Tom, revealed to his social worker, is enacted through the scripting of an over-coded therapeutic relationship, in which, for instance, Tom is calculatingly invited to consider working-through his feelings about the trial, projecting the figure of the 'uneasy' psychologist into the position of the patient (58). 'I was starting to think *I* might consult *him*,' he will tell Danny's social worker (62). Offering Danny the metaphor of permeability to name the latter's sense of confusion between 'what I'm feeling and what other people are feeling,' Tom caps his performance by noting Danny's 'impressive display of self-knowledge' (59). The trap is sprung, and Tom becomes the latest in a line of helpers whom Danny has preyed on by playing up to their desire for progress in the project of rehabilitation. Mrs Greene, the headmaster's wife, is well situated to see what Danny is doing because she has watched her husband invent scores of new lives at Long Garth: 'And you see the really devilish thing? Danny wasn't breaking the rules. They were. He was very, very good at getting people to step across that invisible border' (129).

With the rules undone, the talking cure becomes the vehicle for juxtaposing incompatible elements in contemporary life. It is Angus MacDonald who introduces the distinction between 'raking up the past' to get at the truth, and 'for its own sake' (154). Barker studiously disguises this defence of the literary imagination within a travesty of literary culture, a writers' workshop which is equal to any of the bizarre human rituals acted out in writing classes described by the poet Hugo Williams in his *Times Literary Supplement* column 'Freelancing' (collected as *Freelancing* (1995)). Despite Angus's posturing – 'the whole idea of writing as therapy make me puke' – the pluralism implicit in his methods comes across as a challenge both to the models of human flourishing underpinning the counselling 'industry' and to Tom's current project with Danny. When it comes to the value of talking or writing about the past it isn't a matter of 'the truth', which Angus marks off as a false absolute: 'We're talking about different, and quite often incompatible, versions of it' (155). This formulation captures the novel's presentation of its most salient themes – crime and rehabilitation – as well as those which are relayed from earlier novels, such as masculinity, violence and mental health. The increasingly pressurized interaction between Tom and Danny in their series of chats and sessions is counterpointed with the digressiveness inherent in the temporal scheme of the investigation. The narrative grants to the realm of ideas both an urgent friction and the implacableness of notions which are sedimented and incommensurable.

The question of rehabilitation, and whether human beings can change, is the turbid heart of the sessions. Danny presents himself as someone who'd 'like to' believe in redemption, but this gesture can only be understood in the wake of his accusation of bad faith against the rehabilitation industry:

> 'all sorts of people whose jobs actually depend on a belief that people can change, social workers, probation officers, clinical psychologists' – he smiled – 'psychiatrists, don't really believe it at all.' (52)

Because Danny's provocation – which distracts Tom from entertaining other reasons for his antagonism – is rhetorical, its truth status is irrelevant to its role in the novel's symbolic representation of a divisive society in which pathologies loop through ideals of therapy to reinforce a sense of hopelessness (a contemporary example would be the way diet now operates as coding of social class as biological destiny). Tom's fundamental understanding of behaviour as the learned responses which permit humans to survive in particular environments commits him to the position that to change the individual you must first change the environment. He resists the red rag of Danny's 'logic' of reversion to type by pointing out, reasonably, that 'the old situation might not still be there,' but this model is contradicted by the clinical experience Barker grants him, which by implication correlates conduct disorder with poverty and family dysfunction (53). It is striking that Danny's officer-class/gentleman-farmer origins do not function more powerfully in the novel to reverse this presumption.

The novelist Ford Madox Ford observed that 'the novel has become indispensable to the understanding of life,' and that remains as true now as when the judgement was made in 1930 (Ford, 8). *Border Crossing* does not seek to explain, it puts explanations into motion so that once we see them dramatized, we begin to appreciate where they fit in with the values with which we articulate our lives. We can see that Danny's attempt to substitute explanations for his conduct is a means by which Barker can renew her fictional treatment of the place of violence in the social and cultural order. Where, in the *Regeneration* trilogy, she denaturalized the violence of war by refracting it through psychoanalytic and anthropological frames of reference (to the extent of suggesting that the violence of war is an aspect of human nature), this narrative invites us to view the military, in the guise of a warrior masculinity, as a general model of pathological socialization. The linguistic codes that dominate the novel imply that a society which is relatively immune from the violence of war readily calls forth a symbolism of war in order to identify and explain the civil violence which scars its public and private places. Tom's book on conduct disorder is really a book about child 'warriors', with a 'primitive and exacting' morality centred on 'issues of loyalty, betrayal, rights (theirs), courage, cowardice, reputation, shame' (25). These are not the child soldiers of contemporary third-world conflicts – their participation in military operations would be a national scandal – but the military analogy is a good fit because of the lasting power of the adversary imagery of battle front and home front: 'Nothing much in common with the values of mainstream society'. That the proximal cause is environmental – 'sink housing estates, urban ghettoes' – does nothing to weaken the association when such estates are a no go area, the urban equivalent of no man's land (25, 111).

Danny plays on the warrior motif in his attempt to confound Tom's historical judgement. His account of his childhood represents elaborate variations on current theories about violence and its consequences. Apparently, Danny is offering his father's physical abuse of the young Danny as an explanation, but he carefully avoids voicing that term with its evaluative freight, let alone the entailment of abuse's generational contagion:

> 'So. Were you abused?'
>   'I don't know. Do you think I was?' (96)

Tom is made to do the running here by Danny's qualifications. Danny is equally skilled at displaying icons for his interlocutor to interpret, in order to disguise his designs. His verbal juxtaposition of two portraits, one in a Paddington Bear t-shirt, the other 'wearing a flak-jacket and carrying a gun', channels the account of his father's army career, and his bringing home a frustrated military masculinity, towards a unstated narrative of the child's transformation (90). Another iconic memory is watching war movies, especially Francis Ford Coppola's *Apocalypse Now* (1979). Tom's impatient '[i]sn't that an anti-war movie?' nicely suggests Danny's skill in underplaying his hand. Against the grain of the contemporary autobiography of abusive upbringing, Danny refuses to initiate the diagnosis, challenging Tom to read between the lines of his reserved judgements. He launches the possibility that his father was traumatized by his service in Belfast and the Falklands only to dismiss the syndrome as something which reflects the values of the 'sensitive types' who elaborate it (93). Tom eventually catches up with Danny's ruse, which is more sophisticated than using the father's displaced military violence as an excuse. It is as if Danny has read Tom's drafts, and is presenting a 'warrior' morality in which it is right to kill '[c]hickens, convicted murderers, rabbits, enemy soldiers, farm animals, enemy civilians (in some circumstances), game birds, children (in uniform), burglars, if caught on the premises, and Irishmen, if suspected of being terrorists and providing appropriate warnings had been given' (97). Tom's own construct puts into question his earlier judgement about Danny's capacity to understand that killing is wrong.

Danny will resurface to trouble the characters of Barker's next novel, *Double Vision*, in the person of Peter Wingrave, a character who wants to be therapist and is addicted to giving therapists hell (*Double Vision*, 191). Another recurrence is the 10-year-old Danny's rather dispassionate evaluation of the public framework within which the morality of killing is discussed:

> Thousands of people get killed all the time, all over the world. You know, people look at the telly, and they say, 'Oh, isn't that awful?' But they don't mean it. (31)

The challenge of that 'startling opinion' is amplified into a reconsideration of the role of art in our apprehension of violence.

Another World and *Border Crossing* are linked not only by their dramatization of the violence of boys, but also by their remorseless exploration of the social and cultural shocks which ramify from the eruption of barbarity where it is least supposed to be, in childhood, the age of innocence. There are longer-range connections with the portrayal of systematic domestic violence in the early fiction, and with the trilogy's representation of the world of the hyper-civilized warrior youths whose adolescence ended in Flanders. Taken as a whole, Barker's fiction begins to look like a sustained project of revealing violence where it is occluded and, where it is acknowledged, challenging the terms in which we understand it. *Another World* and *Border Crossing* dramatize themes of the trilogy in the context of contemporary life, provoking us to rethink our assumptions about the pastness of the trauma of war, and the way that trauma is quarantined by the rituals and symbols of remembrance. Her next two fictions focus on the role of the artist in the complex economy of symbols through which violence, past and present, both confronts and 'mystifies' us (Zizek, 3).

6

DOUBLE VISION AND *LIFE CLASS*

In some strange way, the horror flatters attention, it gives to
one's own limited means a spurious resonance.

(Steiner, 32)

Pat Barker's most recent novels, *Double Vision* (2003) and *Life Class*
(2007), are set at what appear to be the margins of modern war,
at either end of what the historian Eric Hobsbawm has called 'the
most murderous century' (Hobsbawm, 1987, 149): Northumbria
in the aftermath of the break-up of Yugoslavia, the Slade School
of Fine Art in the months leading up to the Great War in 1914.
This is not the first time that Barker has chosen protagonists who
are artists, but there is a further reflexive dimension involved in
the creation of the sculptor Kate Frobisher, and the painters Paul
Tarrant, Elinor Brooke and Kit Neville (the latter characters drawing on the historical Slade students Paul Nash, Dora Carrington
and C. R. W. Nevinson). These latest novels are about our vicarious relations to human suffering and, ultimately, about our reading, and her writing, of fictions of military violence such as the
Regeneration trilogy.

The epigraph to *Double Vision* draws together three captions
from Goya's series of etchings of the violence of the Peninsular
War (1808–14), published posthumously as *The Disasters of War*:
'One cannot look at this'; 'I saw it'; and 'This is the truth' (Goya, *Los
Desastres de la Guerra*, nos 23, 44 and 82). In other words: atrocity,
spectacle and witness. These are concepts which Stephen Sharkey

is attempting to compose into a book about 'the ways wars are represented' (57). But they are also compulsions he must resolve if he is to 'heal' himself in rural retirement from a career as war-correspondent. That Goya is 'squatting' over Stephen's project 'like a monstrous jewelled toad' is a double allusion, recalling Larkin's poem about the tyranny of work ('Toads' from *The Less-Deceived* of 1955) but also Shakespeare's *As You Like It*: 'Sweet are the uses of adversity/Which, like the toad, ugly and venomous,/Wears yet a precious jewel in his head' (2.1.12–14). The literal implication of Duke Senior's speech – that pastoral retreat from the city or from professional life is a form of therapy – clearly fit Stephen's Northumbrian refuge, but there is a further and more troubling association. Just as adversity – a 'state of misfortune, distress, trial, or affliction' (*OED*) – holds out moral and sensuous rewards, so images of adversity are associated with both instruction, and, more controversially, with pleasure. The Roman poet Horace wrote in his *Ars Poetica* ('The Art of Poetry', first century BCE) that poetry should mix teaching and entertainment. This conjunction is echoed in the way his third Ode links pleasure and duty as the attributes of patriotic self-sacrifice: *Dulce et decorum est pro patria mori* (It is sweet and proper to die for one's country). This is now remembered as the antithesis of modern incredulity towards lies about slaughter – as exemplified by Wilfred Owen's poem '*Dulce et decorum est*'. But *Double Vision* raises doubts about the uses of witnesses to war, whether documentary or artistic. Are the effects of representing atrocity and war always positive? Or is the depiction of violence yet another violation of the victim, and destined to titillate the onlooker? It is in this sense that *Double Vision* is to be read as a reflection on art's efficacy as an ethical discourse and on Barker's own career as a 'war writer'.

Goya's presence in *Double Vision* is itself a reminder of the referential instability of the imagery of war, and of its multiple functions or effects. Goya anticipates, or even forecloses, modern horrors (which, in a doubled complacence, are often assumed to exceed earlier disasters of war). His etching 'One cannot look at this', wrote Gwyn Williams in the 1970s, 'could be My Lai', a massacre of Vietnamese by American troops in 1968 which fuelled support for the anti-war movement in the United States (Williams, 1). But Goya's work has also been a provocation to excess, as if to reinstall the division of twentieth-century violence and its representations from images of past atrocity which have become familiar, and detoxified, exhibits in our cultural history. This is arguably the case with the Chapman brothers' toy-soldier dioramas based on Goya's *Disasters* (1993), and the same artists' subsequent 'rectified' or defaced version of *Los Desastres de la Guerra* (*Insult to Injury*, 2003). In the era of neo-colonial, asymmetrical war, Philip Shaw has suggested, 'an act of desecration becomes a way of telling the truth,' and the Chapmans' vandalism one of the few remaining options for disrupting the alliance between war and representation (Shaw, 503). Barker's way with Goya is, by contrast, humanist, a defence of art in the face of the hegemony of the photographic and the televisual, which have emerged as both the medium of war, as in Baudrillard's reading of the Gulf War of the Senior George Bush (Baudrillard), and a weapon of war, as in the spectacular destruction of the towers of the World Trade Centre labelled 9/11.

Stephen is not the only character in *Double Vision* who produces representations of violence. The sculptor Kate Frobisher has been commissioned to make a 'huge Christ for the cathedral', a project made difficult both by the burden of traditional representations of Christ, the archetypal sacrificial victim, and by her injuries in a car crash. Kate's double predicament, belated and dependent, itself points to a fault line in the representation of suffering: 'A naked man being tortured is a martyr. A naked woman being tortured is a sadist's wet dream' (149). There is a troubling proximity between the moral and the sensual (or, if you like, duty and desire), and this is at its most paradoxical in the special province of the tutelary representation of violence. This issue is elaborated through the documentary work of Kate's dead husband, the war-photographer Ben, as well as through the creative writing of Peter Wingrave, the studio assistant forced upon her by her accident.

Ben's death in Afghanistan is one of the traumas of which Stephen's book can be thought to be a working through. Stephen had found Ben, shot by a sniper as he composed his last photograph, and brought home this last image of broken Soviet tanks:

> This mass of military debris filled most of the frame, so that from the viewer's angle they seemed to be a huge wave about to break. Behind them was a small white sun, no bigger than a golf ball, veiled in mist. No people. (123)

This is the end of the world, Ben's *'Dies Irae'* (the name of a thirteenth-century hymn describing the Day of Judgement) and a statement about war which appears to transcend time and place. Those familiar with the painting of Paul Nash will recognize his canvas of wrecked Luftwaffe aircraft, *Totes Meer* (Dead Sea), 1940–41, as the original of this fictional photograph. The image compels Stephen to 'find a way to use it' in his book, a book which is scrupulously conceived to disappoint the public appetites his publisher would like to satisfy with salacious anecdotes such as 'Amusing Mass Murderers I Have Met' (118). He believes the image stands for a different effect in war art, not an aesthetic shock but a morally challenging confrontation with war. But the appetite for that which 'one cannot look at' is always kept before us in the novel. It is most wittily invoked in the war-correspondent's self-consciousness about being sick on a fair-ground ride. Machismo is balanced in this episode with a ludic or playful nausea (vertiginous discomfort as a form of entertainment) to underscore the ever-present risks of *Schadenfreude*, of pleasure in another's troubles (194).

Ben is portrayed as a critical photographer, an artist alert to the moral questions raised by a profession which combines the roles of witness, bystander and vicarious perpetrator. Barker alludes to images which are famous in the history of war photography in order to prompt us to reconsider the meaning and value of icons of modern conflict. Ben's photographs of an execution frame 'his own shadow in the shot': 'the shadow says I'm here.' The best-known analogue is Eddie Adams's 1968 photograph of a summary execution by pistol in the streets of Saigon. Once disseminated, this Pulitzer-prize-winning shot was a summary and objective judgement on the regime and character of the Saigon Chief of Police, Nguyen Ngoc Loan. Ben's image, by contrast, has 'exploded the convention' of photographic record, acknowledging that his presence as photographer 'determine[s] what happens next' (123). However, not all his images lay bare the photographer's art in this manner.

Earlier in the narrative, Stephen has a flashback to his discovery of a genitally mutilated girl on a Sarajevo landing. His reactions suggest an incapacity to interpret this corpse, with its staring eyes, as a casualty of war; he pulls down her skirt, then admonishes himself for disturbing a 'crime scene', as if the girl belonged in a scenario of forensic and judicial closure. A second shock is discovering in Ben's archives, a print of the shot of the body with skirt raised, that is a restoration of scene which quotes or re-produces the spectacle the assailants had made of this female body. Stephen 'was shocked on her behalf to see her exposed like this, though, ethically, Ben had done nothing wrong'. Nevertheless, it is as if she has been 'violated twice' (121), anticipating the terms in which Kate connects representations of female suffering with sadistic fantasy. Witness has become confused with the actions and intentions of the perpetrators.

A larger context for this examination of photo-journalism, its determining things, not simply observing them, is 9/11. Ben's role as professional witness is brought to a point of crisis by an event which was intended to symbolize a challenge to the world order, a change of the world:

> That was designed to be a photo-opportunity, and what have I done? I've spent the whole bloody day photographing it . . . . Because we can't escape from the need for a visual record. The appetite for spectacle. And they've used that against us, just as they've used our technology against us. (101)

The instant clichés of the War on Terror are used here to suggest the exorbitance and self-pity of the photographer's self-accusation: feeding the appetite for spectacle, by this argument, produces violence in the form of spectacle. The 'witness turns into an audience' (227). Although many are quick to attribute a meaning to the spectacle of the missing towers – the inauguration of a new era, a war of and on terror – the novel knows this isn't so. Ben's, and Stephen's, ethical dilemma (the tension between showing the truth and the effects of showing it) has been anticipated by Goya.

Ben's witness to violence is juxtaposed with that of Kate's assistant. Peter Wingrave has been a creative writing student and, we will learn, a child murderer: he could very well be Ian Wilkinson (aka Danny Miller) of *Border Crossing*. This is another example of repetition in Barker's oeuvre, reflecting back on the question of the therapist's capacity for insight into his patients, and for engineering change in their behaviour, but also complicating the *roman-à-thèse* about war art. Kate suspects that Peter is the 'headless figure' who appeared in the window of her crashed car before she lost consciousness, a voyeur of the damaged female body (perhaps alluding to Cronenberg's 1996 film of *Crash*, the 1973 novel which its author J. G. Ballard described as a fictional pornography of the technological). Peter's short stories suggest to Stephen an insider's familiarity with carceral institutions, and they remind us of Goya's injunction not to look:

> That was one story he wouldn't be reading twice .... The stories kept slipping into sympathy with the predatory behaviour they attempted to analyse ... it was this ambiguity in the narrator's attitude to predator and prey, rather than the actual events, that made the stories so unsettling. (164)

Peter's fiction is another touchstone with which to judge Ben's photo-journalism, which similarly risks taking up the vantage of the predator. Moreover, Barker has worked this territory herself, notably in the description of the rape and murder of Kath in *Blow Your House Down*, a scenario which the reader may well recognize in Ben's Sarajevo photograph. Just as Barker's earlier manipulation of narrative person and point of view troubles the reader's assumption of distance from sexual violence, so Stephen's paraphrase and interpretation of Peter's grotesque and offensive stories reconfigures the theme of representation. 'Inside the Wire' (which also involves an echo of an earlier Barker novel, as it reprises the seduction of Tom by Danny) dramatizes an audience's projection of its values onto an image or narrative. Art, it is suggested, catches us out in revealing all we are.

Stephen, writing about the Second Gulf War (the 1991 cruise-missile bombardment of Baghdad and 'Desert Storm'), touches on some of the issues raised by Jean Baudrillard (whose polemical claim that this war did not take place was intended to show how far war in the era of electronic media had been transformed into an unequal or asymmetrical contest of representations). Conflict has apparently been reconstituted as an event in the visible spectrum, a (tele)visual effect, with the contradictory result that 'one cannot look at this' (war's casualties) because they are literally rendered imperceptible. The war is broadcast as 'a kind of *son et lumière* display', the bombardment 'acquires the bloodless precision of a video game', while 'the human cost of battle is invisible' (241).

Does this scenario make the photograph which declares 'I saw it' more precious, or is all imagery subsumed to the entertainment industry, and therefore testimony to 'the profound immorality of all images' (Baudrillard, 47)?

Barker asserts a role for art in counteracting this diagnosis with its suspicion of all representations. Kate is prompted into a critique of her dead husband's profession by a small Goya interior, a prison scene composed by a 'compassionate eye' rather than turned into a 'visual record' by the lens.

> Photographs shock, terrify, arouse compassion, anger, even drive people to take action, but does the photograph of an atrocity ever inspire hope? This did. These men have no hope, no past, no future, and yet, seeing this scene through Goya's steady and compassionate eye, it was impossible to feel anything as simple or as trivial as despair. (152–3)

As the philosopher Stanley Cavell has suggested, 'a painting *is* a world; a photograph is *of* the world' (Cavell, 24); the difference Kate insists on is also the difference between a dramatization of the issues of representation and identification, and a treatise on the subject. But Peter's stories lack compassion, and this is why they mimic photography's denotation, 'the detailed observation that implied empathy, and yet, somehow, mysteriously failed to deliver it' (165). The implied autism is a special case of a failure to apperceive the mental states of the persons in the frame, who more easily become objects to be manipulated or staged. In Stephen and Kate's conversation, Goya becomes a touchstone for what each is struggling to work with:

> 'Isn't it amazing, the way he shows rape? You still can't do that now.'
> 'They're not generally keen on an audience.'
> As he spoke he had a flashback to the stairwell in Sarajevo. One of the worst he'd had for quite a while. It's not true, he thought, that images lose their power with repetition, or not automatically true anyway. That memory, which had now become subtly different because Ben's photograph had been grafted on to it, never failed to shock. (155)

There is something odd about the syntax of Kate's diagnosis of current taboos, a slippage in temporalities that contains a condescending, presentist assumption that we are the first generation who have advanced beyond squeamishness and prudery to face reality in the raw. Traumatic memory – unintegrated flashbacks – has become a capacious metaphor for the counter-argument, and for the unassimilable in historical and social crisis, and its traces in culture. Here Barker collapses the metaphor with Steven's surprisingly crude joke, which reveals the extent to which being witness to an event and audience to a representation are becoming inseparable.

In *Regarding the Pain of Others* (2003), the veteran critic Susan Sontag asserted that '[b]eing a spectator of calamities taking place in another country is a quintessential modern experience' (Sontag, 2004, 16). Not just the most murderous century, but the century of remote spectacle. We could approach *Double Vision* as a story about Sontag's thesis, first presented as an Amnesty lecture in Oxford in 2001. The novel draws on some of the same exhibits as Sontag, not least the example of Goya, and it dramatizes Sontag's contention that there is more going on than we might think in the assumption 'that if the horror could be made vivid enough, most people would finally take in the outrageousness, the insanity of war' (12). Noting that 'photography as shock therapy' (13) is part of the same economy of images as shock 'as a leading stimulus of consumption' (20), Sontag raises a moral question that the ubiquity of such images may seem to preclude:

> there is shame as well as shock in looking at the close-up of real horror. Perhaps the only people with the right to look at images of suffering of this extreme order are those who could do something to alleviate it . . . . The rest of us are voyeurs, whether or not we mean to be. (38)

This, rather than Sontag's attempts to characterize photography in terms of witness, artistry and evidence, is the crux of Barker's book.

As much as it is concerned with the making of art, *Double Vision* is concerned too with its consumption, with the fact that a work of art is incomplete until it is read or looked at. It is in this sense that Stephen's crazy attempt to save Ben, recalled in the last pages, is validated. He replicates Ben's wager for the image – 'your life – *for that?*' – first by seeing what Ben had seen – 'a wave breaking. A sun so white it might have been the moon' – and then by bringing back the 'last photographs' (305–6). In the case of Kate's Christ, the situation appears more complex; the artist is haunted by the voyeur (whereas Stephen's memory as witness is haunted by Ben's visual 'documentation'), who is also studio assistant, mimic and finally audience. It is not only that something of Peter has gone into the figure – which 'hasn't forgotten anything . . . . Betrayal, torture. Murder' – but that his looking upon the figure has finished it (292). 'The figure seemed different, though really it was her way of seeing it that had changed . . . . Because somebody else had seen it . . . . There was a life here now that no longer depended on her' (300–1). The Christ has become 'a thing apart' at the moment it has an audience. That Peter claims the Christ is 'about memory' is ironical in proportion to our remembering Danny in *Border Crossing*, of whom Peter is a tantalizing revenant.

The account of the work's completion is itself a repetition of the scene in which Kate watched Peter, she thinks, 'destroying her Christ' but actually '[p]retending to be her'. But his dressing up as the artist doesn't, as she first rationalizes, have the effect of ritually 'stealing her power'; it permits her to apprehend her creative power (178). Peter has made no chisel marks, but the figure is 'Beaten up. Somebody with a talent for such things had given him a right going over.' This is her work, so '[i]f it looked different, it must be because her way of seeing it had changed.' These are her marks, not his, yet the disturbing traces of 'what happens in history' still seem to her to be associated with his mime and not her imagination (180–1). The problem of where such images come from appears to be more pressing in the case of Peter, whose stories are treated by Stephen as symptoms rather than an artistic vision, evidence of the writer's behaviour – 'Torture. Mental and physical. Murder' – rather than his themes. Peter, who shares Danny's active resistance to discourses of therapy, has strategies for outflanking claims that his writing can only be first-personal memory, and Justine's father, Alec, the latest agent of Peter's rehabilitation, is his spokesman:

> he's interested in [stalking]. Because it's a pattern of behaviour that's been known about for centuries and has only recently been declared pathological. He's interested in the way psychiatry's expanded and laid claim to previously . . . neutral, or, . . . anyway non-pathological areas of human behaviour. (212–13)

Whether her 'deranged double' reveals anything about Kate, perhaps that she has a 'dark side' such as Peter defensively claims as the source of his characters, is an issue Barker refracts through the novel (it is one meaning elicited by the title, *Double Vision*), even as her characters try to untangle the complex relations of life and art (179, 199). Stephen's comparison of Peter's work with Ian McEwan's is typical of the possibilities Barker sets in motion. McEwan is invoked here both as the author of remorseless tales of violence and perversion (*First Love, Last Rights*, 1975) and as an influence. Stephen is confirmed in his fears about Peter by the latter's image of literary influences as skins to be worn and then sloughed off. The stories are thus construed as a memory, confirming the continuity of selfhood which Peter's passing with a new identity is all about denying. Stephen's opting to deal with what is disturbing in his reading experience by locating it either in Peter's life or in the imitation of McEwan alludes to the author's own allusive practice (McEwan's example presides over the beginning of *Border Crossing*) and to her own tarrying with the shocking. Her novels complement and indeed muddy their conceptual intricacy with visceral impacts, simultaneously remodelling received ideas and making us wince. In interview in 1992, Barker called her 'psychopathic figures' (looking back to *Union Street* and *Blow Your House Down*) 'emblems of violence . . . rather than actual characters' (Nixon, 15). Peter retains something of this emblematic quality, in part because Barker won't reveal him: 'he is a dark patch in an overall picture' (Monteith, 30). He is thus the 'deranged double' in so far as his presence is what facilitates the projection of the other characters' fears, and which helps them demarcate the realm of the human from 'that in human nature which we find it impossible to accept' (Monteith, 23). In parallel with Ben's 9/11 photographs, which Barker has called 'the image of trauma for which there is no talking cure' (which comes pretty close to saying trauma is 'non-pathological' human experience), Peter is the 'character' who is constituted of those proclivities – voyeurism, violence and lack of compassion – which the others cannot integrate into their accounts of themselves (Brannigan, 383). As such, he's also an emblem of the novelist's cruel inventions.

Double Vision isn't confined to the realm of the virtual, to the spectatorship of the image with which Stephen's books is concerned. It is striking that Barker has recalled that the composition of *Double Vision* 'started almost with another book – the one Stephen is writing in the novel,' as if the fictional work supplanted Sontag's historical one, which is duly acknowledged in the 'Author's Note' (Monteith, 29). Stephen is also witness to apparently unmediated events. While war is remote, and he must meditate on the morality and efficacy of trying to bring war home in the form of images, what brings the essence of war home is violence in the form of crime. We have noted Barker's fascination with the way society demarcates permitted violence and that which is outlawed, an interest which has led from the family as a zone of violence via the streets to the Western Front. The West's way of going to war has developed significantly since then, and with greater pace since the 1970s. The asymmetry of contemporary Western war making (precisely what Baudrillard meant by its non-existence), in particular the inadmissibility of friendly casualties, that is war is a cost to be borne by tax-payers, but not directly by the subjects or citizens, has been accompanied by progress in criminalizing acts of war (but not, definitely not, outlawing war itself).

The Milosevic trial in the Netherlands in 1992 is Stephen's professional opportunity to cover a war criminal. But the trial is a contest of representations in which images are suddenly without denotative power, and the captions are all: ' "And this," said Milosevic the next day, embarking with some enthusiasm on a gruesome game of Snap, "is the severed head of a Serbian child" ' (130). The spectacle of indictment is dysfunctional, for Milosevic is the sole beneficiary: 'the dead had been made to work overtime, appearing as victims in the propaganda of both sides,' the court officials and audience 'ashamed of their inability to go on feeling' (130). Yet the trial makes visible what had been invisible during the genocidal and humanitarian military campaigns in 'the former' Yugoslavia, when war had been 'sanitized', had reverted to 'sepia tint': '[h]uman bodies baked like dog turds in the sun,' and like dog turds went unregarded (131). Photographic witness is subordinated to targeting and propaganda – 'puffs of brown smoke ... under the cross-hairs of the precision sights' – but worse is to come. The ritual drama of indictment and correction which is finally staged in the front-page photo which 'showed the chief prosecutor ... laughing in triumph as the ex-dictator, a shadowy figure with bowed shoulders, was escorted to his seat' (135). But it never happened: the triumph is a product of the neutrality of the lens, the ingenuity of the photo-editor and the credulity of the newspaper reader. The meaning of the event is only arrived at when its representation is read. There's more at issue than 'photography as the guarantor of reality' (135). Photography becomes a weapon governments can use against their own, ever better educated populace. David Simpson has explained just how the 'embedding' of photo-journalists in military units functions as a mode of censorship: 'The wager is that a cynical and self-absorbed populace will by now be quite used to accepting the potential for deception attached to all photographic documentation of suffering' (Simpson, 26).

By contrast with this serially mediated staging of international justice, Stephen is involved in a drama which touches him much more acutely, and goes someway to account for why regarding the pain of others requires more than a powerful and truthful image. His witness of the eruption of violence into the Adamic world of Stephen and his girlfriend Justine playing at home and family is literally the result of a difficulty in writing about what happens when those dog-turd corpses become invisible. Stephen, disconcerted by 'wars designed to ensure that fear and pain never came home', breaks off to walk the hills and looking down on home – like Coleridge striding the Quantocks and imaging the rapine of invading Napoleonic soldiers in his poem 'Fears in Solitude' – sees Justine heading for a rendezvous with the burglars loading up his brother's telly. That the *mise-en-scène* is the stuff of cinematic cliff-hanger melodrama – 'even if he ran till his heart and lungs burst, he still wouldn't get there in time' – is precisely the point. This is Stephen's test, and as such it is appropriate that it is conducted at once in a state of disorientation *and* of media-primed readiness.

> He went over the story he'd told the police, and then the other story: the one he hadn't needed to tell because – thank God – it wasn't relevant. Locked in his brain, though, was the truth. All the way down the hillside he'd had flashbulbs exploding in his head. So many raped and tortured girls – he needed no imagination to picture what might be happening to Justine. It would not have surprised him to find her lying like a broken doll at the foot of the stairs, her skirt bunched up around her waist, her eyes staring. Years of impacted rage had gone into the blow he'd aimed at the back of the burglar's head. (250)

The 'truth' is Stephen's capacity for violence (the burglar's broken bone needs to be explained to the Police). Violence brought home brings home violence witnessed, to the point of producing what is known as a 'proportionate response', proportionate, Stephen thinks, not to burglary but to war. Justine, victim not witness, would disagree: when 'her face exploded with pain' she would not have been in a position to discriminate between her situation and the ones Stephen doesn't have to imagine. The description of Stephen's behaviour here is a component in a more resonant conjunction. This is the way the novel brings together violence mediated, a ubiquitous and tranquilizing spectator event (Stephen's fears, we note, are illuminated by flashbulbs, as if they are already framed by media attention) and violent action, in particular the channelling of emotion into a physical insult. The novel's conclusion complicates all manner of relationships which have been patiently expounded both through Stephen's work on his book, and through Barker's evocation of examples of war iconography, in particular the oppositions between witness and agent, and between audience and event. The novel poses again and again the question of what states of mind does viewing atrocity place us in. Its answers range from the outrage which is channelled towards justice to the voyeurism of Peter and of the audiences of news casts (Justine refuses to watch). The labelling of these responses as proper or improper is confounded by the forensic instability of representations. But the final scene introduces a further complexity as it invites us to consider violence observed issuing in a violent response. The moral equivocation in an act of contemplation tending towards the aesthetic confronts the moral primitivism of vengeance, which ramify with the novel's presentation of the trial of Milosevic. In *Double Vision* Pat Barker risks a melodramatic device to ensure that our vision is doubled back on itself, in a reflexive variation on the theme of the iconography of violence: 'One cannot look at this'; 'I saw it'; 'This is the truth'.

LIFE CLASS: 'IT WOULD JUST BE A FREAK SHOW'

In 1990, Samuel Hynes, literary critic and a Second World War veteran USAF pilot, published *A War Imagined*, a cultural history which treated the First World War as not only the 'great' military and political event of the early twentieth century, but 'also the great imaginative event'. Hynes was interested in the processes by which a 'Myth of the War' was defined in the 1920s, not least because of its abiding influence: 'It continues to be accepted in our own time. In novels, films, television documentaries, popular histories, the story remains the same; we live still in that myth' (Hynes, ix, xi).

We have seen how *Regeneration* intervenes in that 'war imagined', working against the grain of '[o]ur war . . . the myth of the war, based in literature and art, that we credit as truth,' as well as, necessarily, reproducing it (Hynes, 153). The intelligibility of the trilogy is conditional on invoking the Myth which 'remains a powerful imaginative force . . . in the shaping not only of our conceptions of what war is, but of the world we live in' (Hynes, 469). Re-imagining depends then on a negotiation between a writer and a reader's cultural experience, an intertextual network which is broader than the direct transactions between writers, such as allusion and imitation.

Hynes argues that '*our* war' begins with wartime dissent, such as the offensive poems Siegfried Sassoon published in the *Cambridge Magazine* in 1916. Another example of the emergence of 'our' discourse of war is the wartime acclaim of the work of the English modernist painter C. R. W. Nevinson. In the case of this war artist, as with the anti-heroic poetry of 1916, the nature of the Great War comes to be represented not so much by a new style as by the fact of a change of style itself. This is apparent in Hynes's reading of the reception of Nevinson's experimental and culturally marginal work. The radical style of this futurist-influenced painting only became intelligible to critics when war changed reality:

> the war was Modernist . . . the violence and the mechanism of pre-war experimental art had been validated as perceptions of reality by the war itself. Not only validated, but made necessary.
>
> (Hynes, 164)

This viewpoint might seem at odds with Hynes's general thesis (modernism is far from being the dominant aesthetic of 'our war'). But then it is rooted in another element of the Myth which has proved particularly difficult to demystify, namely the idea that the war determines its own representation (as in 'the war was Modernist'). Thus the 'reality of war', an epistemological grail within post-war culture, necessitates the abandonment of earlier idealizations. This view of the genesis of modern war literature and art underwrites the authority of the creators of these dissenting representations of war, and later guarantees their centrality in our culture. These representations are not to be thought of as the products of an individual vision (the work of Sassoon or Owen is inconceivable in these terms) but as 'the truth of war', a new universal for an age of violence.

Life Class is Pat Barker's return to the semiotic and somatic terrain of our war. This time the hospital that can 'show you what war is' is not an asylum, but resembles the shambles in Remarque's *All Quiet on the Western Front*, where the bodies of combatants are patched up behind the lines, a stage on which the phallic, armoured, warrior male is revealed to be soft, perishable flesh:

> Shrapnel had come through from the back and severed the penis at the base. As they watched, urine welled up from the hole in his groin, hot acid spreading over raw flesh. The man arched his back and groaned again. (136)

The figure is Dantean, one of the wretched portrayed in a hell of self-consumption, but the overtones are aesthetic: the body's fluids etch pain on flesh. The scenario evokes the machinery of torture which inscribes the sentence on the body in Kafka's 'In the Penal Colony' (1919) but it also points in the opposite direction, to the artistic techniques used by William Blake. The relief-etched plates in *The Songs of Experience* – in which the verse and illustration are cut with acid – portray the body bound to the savage disciplines of economics and war. These associations are important because *Life Class* is a novel about art, not war, even though art is addressed in terms of the pressures of war, and the pressures exerted by Hynes's Myth of the War.

Literary critics have, for some time, been fascinated by the apparent reciprocity between war and art. One of the most potent ideas in Paul Fussell's *The Great War and Modern Memory* is that of the Great War as 'a literary war', one in which unfamiliar experience was conceived on the model of literary precedents, whether the King James Bible and Bunyan, or the poetry of Hardy and Housman. The business of inhabiting the Western Front and imprinting it with the signs that made it both navigable and mockable (e.g., overlaying London street names on the trench system, and anglicizing continental place names, such as 'Wipers' for Ypres) created a world of uncanny juxtapositions. *Life Class* reflects these cultural motifs and in doing so suggests that art, in these times, cannot be quarantined from war, even if its role in wartime is far from obvious to its practitioners. The title puns on the name of the lesson, the life class, in which Slade students practice drawing human models (Teresa, Paul's lover, is one such). But life itself is a kind of class too, in which Paul and Kit and Elinor are trying out their selves and their aspirations, in particular learning how to be artists after Art School. But the biggest differences between life and the classroom are the compulsions and risks provoked by the body when it is no longer safely on a pedestal, framed by the rules of art. In fact Elinor's performances of intimacy create the safest arena for Paul's sexuality, which, as Barker has put it, is 'wildly out of sync' with his capacity for getting close emotionally, and thus a correlative of his art (Brannigan, 389).

There are other associations to the opening scene of the novel, from which the title derives, and these, echoing the rhetoric of disillusionment in war literature, involve ironic prolepsis or anticipation. The 'naked woman on the dias' Paul has drawn will, when Paul's artistic goals are modified by his experience of war, ultimately be supplanted by the figures of the male nurse and the patient, the former 'a white-swaddled mummy intent on causing pain', the latter stripped of skin, 'a blob of tortured nerves' (3, 203). The one is armoured, both by his mask and gown and by his professional, clinical detachment; the other is more than naked. It is also notable that in the hospital painting, the figure of the artist has been brought inside the frame, picking up on the handling of the idea of witness in *Double Vision*. Another chain of ironic associations leads from still life (what you draw when you cannot afford a model) via the French term for such a composition, *nature mort*, to Paul Nash's *Totes Meer*, the Second World War painting by the veteran war artist of the Great War which is recreated in *Double Vision* as Ben Frobisher's last image. Art's relations to still life/dead nature (the anxiety behind Keats's 'Ode on a Grecian Urn') anticipate the aesthetic dilemmas of war art, of both the recruitment of art to war and the broadening of the canons of art to incorporate 'the reality of war'.

These issues are coded even more suggestively in the incidental detail of the scene with which the novel opens. The segregation of the sexes 'when the naked body was on display' will be reproduced on the battlefield, though not in the field hospitals where women work besides men on broken bodies. Tonks's inspection of the students' work blends suggestions of a bullying, noisy military authority designed to emasculate its subjects, and military ordnance, designed to pulverize men:

> For God's sake, man, look at that arm. It's got no more bones in it than a sausage. Your pencil's blunt, your easel's wobbly, you're working in your own light and you seem to have no grasp of human anatomy at all.

One of Paul Tarrant's figure drawings is likened to 'blancmange' (4). From 1917, Tonks would be involved in reconstructive surgery, helping to put the bone back in the blancmange of shattered and ripped faces, by drawing the wounds of patients for the pioneer plastic surgeon Harold Gillies, at Queen's Hospital, Sidcup (Tonks had himself been trained as a surgeon before appointment to the Slade). Paul's progress to the Front as nurse and ambulance driver will make him a war artist, confronting the problem of exhibiting images of others' pain. The Antiques Room at the Slade is another such relay, this time from the Greco-Roman heroic figure to the shambles of the Western Front: 'decapitated heads, limbless torsos, amputated arms and legs. Like an abattoir without the blood' (12). Wilfred Owen, long before he was a war poet, greeted the outbreak of war as a calamity of the spirit, with the body only an afterthought:

> I am furious with chagrin to think that the Minds which were to have excelled the civilization of ten thousand years, are being annihilated – and bodies, the product of aeons of Natural Selection, melted down to pay for political statues.
>
> (Owen, *Selected Letters*, 119)

The plasticity of the body in war is imagined with an unflinching foreshortening as the means to the production of memorials, flesh literally moulded into the monumental forms which narrate and substantiate State history. The body is central to Barker's story about the transactions between art and war, not only the body 'melted down', but the body which Owen doesn't for a moment envisage, in his detachment as a civilian overseas, the body of the artist. Paul's enlistment medical (he is tubercular, unfit for military service) is a reprise of the parade of flesh in the life class at the Slade, which will soon be turned into a military hospital (113, 149).

The way *Life Class* anticipates war with these ironic prolepses is essentially different from Sassoon's pre-echoes in *Memoirs of a Fox-Hunting Man* which undercut the naïvety of the disguised autobiographical subject with intimations of his illusion-shattering destiny. Barker is trying to create a distance from the default assumptions of our anti-war culture by, as it were, getting in before the sedimentation of the Myth, and in particular the assumption that art should address military violence as the vehicle of a moral and humane opposition to war: another demonstration of the fact that 'you don't want a preexisting myth in a novel' (Stevenson, 176). For instance, war in this novel is not primarily represented in terms of a narrative of disillusionment but of a threat to the continuation of civilian mores, a 'great steel shutter' (110). Granted, the arc of disappointment can be traced in Paul's progress. We could, for example, note Paul's 'glee' (a word already marked out by its remarkable use in Owen's poem on the joys of combat, '*Apologia pro poemate meo*') at driving off the predatory businessman in the park, an episode couched in mock-chivalric terms. This victory contrasts with his consciousness of the 'world [shrunk] to a few yards of muddy ground' when Teresa's estranged husband Halliday bludgeons him in the livery stables. Perhaps to reinforce this contraction, London has mutated into a claustrophobic St Petersberg, the two scenes clearly echoing Raskolnikov's interference with the man-about-town who is preying on a drunken girl, and the dream of the beating of a horse (*Crime and Punishment*, Part 1, Chapters 4 and 5). Dostoyevsky's novel about the meaning of suffering is an apposite reference point for a story which addresses the apparently meaningless suffering of the Great War. '*Shotvarfet*' was the verdict of Hallett at the end of *The Ghost Road*, a judgement on the war enunciated not by a human voice but reiterated as a whisper from out of 'the suppurating wound left by the rifle bullet. The hernia cerebri pulsated, looking like some strange submarine form of life, the mouth of a sea anemone perhaps' (*Ghost Road*, 264). This association of suffering with the loss of voice is the central conceit of T. S. Eliot's *The*

Waste Land (1922), but one contradicted by the ideal of the war poet as participant witness, 'watching their sufferings that I may speak of them' (Owen, *Letters*, 351). Barker has created a powerfully disorienting image for this loss, as Paul is kicked unconscious: 'The sounds jerking out of him seemed to come from the boot not his mouth' (68). The idea that the body is muted to the extent that its articulacy, its capacity to forge meaning out of experience, has been arrogated to the weapon, is a disturbing reflection on the systematic operations of politics, economics and language which, in a state of war, have their foundations in piles of bodies. The image distills Elaine Scarry's insights into the alienation of suffering from the 'body in pain' to substantiate the state's self-descriptions, which is a ubiquitous feature of discourses of war, and Orwell's vision of uninterrupted totalitarian power in *Nineteen Eighty-Four*: O'Brien offers Winston Smith an icon of a future in which it will not be possible to speak out in opposition, 'a boot stamping on a human face – for ever' (Orwell, 215).

The arc of disillusionment might also be traced over Paul's promotion from nurse to ambulance driver, the realization of an ambition that ironically incapacitates him, making him a stretcher case. Getting his fellow nurse Lewis to an ambulance is the last act of the carer before he is turned into one of the pugnacious subjects of emergency medical attention: 'He fought them, deaf, mad, blind, covered in blood he didn't know was his own' (235). But despite these repetitions of the narrative trajectory central to the Myth, war is not the dominant conception of reality in the novel, and war does not trump all other values. So, where the *Regeneration* trilogy motivated war's echoes throughout the social order as levers with which to reconfigure the proportions of its representation (e.g., promoting the home front), *Life Class* tends rather to make war an echo of its protagonists' immature goals. Paul distances himself from the 'excitement' of 1914 – 'I suppose . . . they all feel they're caught up in history' – and is thus dissociated from the idea of war artists 'chained to a historical event', as Philip Larkin summarized the idea of the poets made by the war (110; Larkin, 159). '[W]ar was a compendium of trivial matters,' Paul thinks, not an apocalypse but something close to 'the endless snubbing and nagging of war', which Patrick Hamilton characterized in his 1947 novel of the Second World War Home Front, *The Slaves of Solitude* (Hamilton, 100). For Elinor, war is just that, 'a single bullying voice shouting all the other voices down', a monologism which she resents (116). If none of the characters seems to rise to the occasion in the way that Sassoon and Owen do in *Regeneration*, this serves to focus our attention on the consumption of, rather than myths of the production of, representations of war.

The handling of sex is a good example of the way Barker insinuates war into the lives of her characters, rather than coding its ubiquity. Elinor's real attraction for Paul is not her flirtatious but really defensive 'air of intimacy' (itself an interesting parallel to the issues of medical sympathy and compassion in the novel) but the boyish mode of her unadapted, unshielded self: 'With her cropped hair and straight shoulders she looked like a young soldier striding along, something of the person she might be when she was alone' (13). This collocation of marching and individuality is paradoxical: the more usual association of the soldier marching is with the subordination of self to a dehumanizing discipline, as in Nevinson's Giacomo Balla-like '*Returning to the Trenches*' (1914), Mark Gertler's 'Merry-Go-Round' (1916) or Isaac Rosenberg's poem 'Marching – as Seen from the Left File' (Walsh, 115; Rosenberg, 123–4). And indeed the orthodox image – soldiers as a mechanical mass – is precisely what Paul will later report to Elinor (197). The spell cast on him by her 'shockingly cropped head' (what Elinor means by it is an affiliation to painting) has two concomitants in the narrative, one homoerotic, notably the love Paul discovers in mourning Lewis, the other, the entwining of the erotic and war (31). The equation of sex and fear marks out Barker's rewriting of Emma Bovary's famous cab ride in Rouen, where she turns the sexual encounter into a species of close-quarters combat (the whites of the eyes are a traditional motif for such scary proximity) during which a clasp of hands is 'a respite from terror' (170). By contrast, Elinor enters the 'forbidden' war zone on her own terms – the real nurses 'needed the war and she didn't' (166). Sex and also the ties of a socialized intimacy are the real threat. That Paul's 'platonic' relationship with the prostitute is destined to end in penetration ('a small, unimportant murder') seems a judgement on his desire to possess Elinor (231). The association of sex and wounding is heavily coloured in: 'a room that seemed to be all pink and shiny, like intestines' is echoed in the subsequent scene of Paul's wounding, where the sight of '[o]ne man lying on the ground cradling his intestines in his arms as tenderly as a woman nursing a sick child' itself recalls Elinor's break-through painting of the mother 'who seemed to melt into her child' (164). The dualities of tender touches and violent blows, of the loving or clinical probing of the body's interior spaces, of maternal care and patriotic duty complicate the divisions with which we are accustomed to understand the war.

By the end of the novel, Elinor is mixing with the same Bloomsbury set – 'You'd have to be a full-blown conchie to get in there' – members of which had urged Sassoon to make his protest. In Aldous Huxley's *Crome Yellow* (1921), his postwar satire of Ottoline Morel's Garsington, Bloomsbury's countryhouse retreat, Mr Scogan (the novel's version of Garsington's pacifist philosopher, Bertrand Russell) offers a coolly detached account of suffering in war:

> Screams of pain and fear go pulsing through the air at the rate of eleven hundred feet per second. After traveling for three seconds they are perfectly inaudible. These are distressing facts; but do we enjoy life any less because of them? Most certainly we do not. We feel sympathy, no doubt; we represent to ourselves imaginatively the sufferings of nations and individuals and we deplore them. But, after all, what are sympathy and imagination? Precious little, unless the person for whom we feel sympathy happens to be closely involved in our affections; and even then they don't go very far. And a good thing too; for if one had an imagination vivid enough and a sympathy sufficiently sensitive really to comprehend and to feel the sufferings of other people, one would never have a moment's peace of mind. A really sympathetic race would not so much as know the meaning of happiness. But luckily, as I've already said, we aren't a sympathetic race. At the beginning of the war I used to think I really suffered, through imagination and sympathy, with those who physically suffered. But after a month or two I had to admit that, honestly, I didn't. And yet I think I have a more vivid imagination than most. One is always alone in suffering; the fact is depressing when one happens to be the sufferer, but it makes pleasure possible for the rest of the world.
>
> (Huxley, 89)

Scogan's insistence that 'sympathy and imagination' travel much less far than the sounds of suffering (their range, he alleges, may be no further than the edge of the bed, or the boundary of the family) appears callous. In fact, echoing George Eliot's observation in *Middlemarch* (1871–72) that with keener feeling 'we would die of that roar which lies on the other side of silence,' Huxley has merely presented an un-idealized account of empathy. What gives the passage its special charge – so that in comparison with Eliot's affiliation with a humanity 'wadded with stupidity' it strikes us as an egotistical withholding of natural affections – is its reference to suffering in war (rather than 'all ordinary human life') (Eliot, 194). Mr Scogan's attitude might strike us as doubly elitist, rejecting fellow feeling with the fallen, and with all those who are convinced that they are capable of compassion, but it also assumes an indifferent universe. Incapacity in vicarious or imaginative suffering makes the actually suffering unreachably remote, and their lonely pain becomes the guarantee of the world's happiness. This is a psychological extrapolation of the trench poets' motif of an epistemic abyss between soldiers and civilians, a model of insensibility which explains how life is possible at all in a violent age. But viewed from the perspective of the human in pain, it is a nightmare, the equivalent of being buried alive. Versions of this question about compassion (or for Wilfred Owen, 'pity') are encountered throughout *Life Class*, in a more understated way than in *Double Vision*. It lies behind Elinor's insistence that the war is unimportant, doesn't matter very much, which is both an effort at a strident aesthetic principle and a symptom of her anxiety about her brother, posted to France.

Most significantly, the very possibility of vicarious suffering and of sympathy is bound up with the idea of war art, and the conviction that the reality of war must be shown to those who have not encountered it directly. Indeed, an early and central motif of the literature of war post-1914 is that knowledge of that reality cannot be, but must be, broadcast beyond the community of combatants. As a nurse, Paul's decisions, for instance, about the changing of dressings may exacerbate pain:

> Speed would have been more merciful, but risked doing further damage. He clenched his teeth as if he were in pain, though the pain was not his and never could be. (136)

Whether Paul's grimace is an empathic miming of pain behaviour, or the rictus of clinical detachment, he cannot compensate for adding to the load of pain by sharing it. Writing 60 years after

Huxley, the philosopher Elaine Scarry has observed that 'another person's physical pain . . . may seem to have the remote character of some deep subterranean fact' or be 'as distant as . . . interstellar events'.

> Whatever pain achieves, it achieves in part through its unsharability, and it ensures this unsharability through its resistance to language. (5–6)

Paul nevertheless experiences an intense pressure to resist the way both professional decorum and representational repertoires abet the disappearance of pain, a dilemma symbolized by standing orders which appear to hinder humane treatment in order to preserve both materiel and warlike appearances: '[t]he military authorities say uniforms must be preserved at all costs' (129). The presence of the uninitiated Lewis reawakens senses blunted by clinical necessity: 'I start *seeing* it all again through his eyes' (147). Lewis complicates Paul's reactions in other ways, adding to the roll call of powerful dialogues of initiation in the literature about the Great War, from *Journey's End* through Susan Hill's novel *Strange Meeting* (1971). The confusion of his own and Lewis's responses is like being 'crowded out of his own mind', a usurpation which raises more difficult questions in relation to the wounded: 'In the face of their suffering, isn't it self-indulgent to think about his own feelings?' (145). Out of such thoughts a model of war art will emerge.

When Elinor visits militarized France, she doesn't want to know about the war, but whether Paul is still working. Nursing is inessential: is he drawing?

> 'Oh, people at the hospital. Patients.' His tone hardened. 'That's what I *see*. Though I don't know what the point of it is. Nobody's going to hang that sort of thing in a gallery.'
> 'Why would you want them to?'
> 'Because it's there. *They're* there, the people, the men. And it's not right their suffering should just be swept out of sight.'
> 'I'd have thought it was even less right to put it on the wall of a public gallery. Can't you imagine it? People peering at other people's suffering and saying, "Oh my *dear*, how perfectly *dreadful*" – and then moving on to the next picture. It would just be a freak show. An arty freak show.' (175–6)

The facts of suffering mandate the representation of suffering. But there is nothing about suffering that determines how its representation will be received.

But Elinor's argument isn't ultimately what it appears to be, a case against the exploitation of other's suffering – 'you can't use people like that' – but one against the denigration of art to the status of a relay for historical and biological disaster.

> The truth is, it's been imposed on us from the outside. You would never have chosen it and probably the men in the hospital wouldn't either. It's unchosen, it's passive, and I don't think that's a proper subject for art. (176)

Patients may be passive, but artists should be agents, exerting power, rather than being the instruments of external forces. Students of Great War poetry may recognize here the notorious but widely misunderstood argument which W. B. Yeats employed in his 1936 *Oxford Book of Modern Verse* to justify the exclusion of poems by Wilfred Owen. Yeats drew on Matthew Arnold's act of self-censorship concerning what he came to view as 'morbid' and 'painful' representations of suffering 'which finds no vent in action' (Schweizer, 107). As Fran Brearton has argued, Yeats's case that 'passive suffering is not a theme for poetry' reflects a longer-range reading of English–Irish literary traditions: 'The English ... have no sense of tragedy ... pity ... has taken its place' (Brearton, 52–3). Yeats's position appears the acme of an ivory-tower, modernist aloofness in contrast with the political engagement of Owen, and the incoherence of the latter's claim 'Above all I am not concerned with Poetry' has all too readily been overlooked. In fact, Yeats's view that war is the enemy of art (Brearton, 50) is an assessment of the consequences of getting 'too near', of the commitment to 'plead the suffering' of servicemen, and of moral choices supplanting aesthetic ones, so that the artist is 'under the shadow of other men's minds'(quoted in Brearton, 51–2). Barker has opened out a dialogue where in literary history there has sedimented an intransigent opposition between Yeats's paradoxical (even absurd) judgement and Owen's cultural centrality. But bringing Paul's war experience and sense of the porousness of the boundaries of his sensibilities ('crowded out of his own mind') into contact with Elinor's refusal to take the war seriously

serves to emphasize what separates them. She refuses to imagine the landscape of war 'churned up . . . by marching feet' because
'*this* was the reality. Grass, trees, pools full of reflected sky, somewhere in the distance a curlew calling' (167). Paul remains loyal
to the same conception of nature and to an art grounded in landscape: 'you didn't do people . . . your nudes didn't look human'
(176). This affiliation is sustained in the knowledge of its apparent
heartlessness:

> close to the front line where the land on either side of the road is
> ruined – pockmarked, blighted, craters filled with foul water, splin-
> tered trees, hedges and fields gouged out – I realized I felt the horror
> of that landscape almost more than I feel for the dying . . . . the human
> body decays and dies in some more or less disgusting way whether
> there's a war or not, but the land we hold in trust. (176, 198)

But his art is changing under pressure of war. His painting of the
treatment of a gangrenous wound, or rather of 'causing pain' to 'a
blob of tortured nerves'

> looked as if it had been painted by somebody else . . . . It had an author-
> ity that he didn't associate with his stumbling, uncertain, inadequate
> self. It seemed to stand alone. Really, to have nothing much to do with
> him. (203)

Is this the impersonality of art (in T. S. Eliot's formula, an escape
from emotion) or is it the Myth of war art, history manifesting
itself through the artists who are chained to war?

An encounter with Kit Neville, Paul's rival for Elinor, leads to the
restatement of the dilemmas surrounding war art as a 'Faustian
pact', in other words a bargain in which the artist sells his integrity
(212). Paul describes his dislike for his 'best' painting in these
terms, as if it is not his work; the feverish fantasy that his infection
was caught from the brush with which he represented trauma, not
the scalpel with which he was treating a gangrenous wound, reinforces the idea that war is a threat to art. The idea recurs when he
meets the publicly acclaimed Kit Neville in London. The artist who
saw war as a 'painting opportunity' is now intent on refashioning
his career in the post-war art world (119).

I think that once the bloody war's over nobody's going to want to look at anything I paint . . . . it's a Faustian pact. I get all the attention for a few months, however long the bloody thing lasts, but once it's over – *finish*. Nobody wants to look at a nightmare once they've woken up. (239)

This projection looks as idiosyncratic at Yeats's verdict on Owen, because looking at the nightmare has become for us a cultural norm. The difference between Neville's anxiety about the market (paintings that are not looked at because they are not in vogue) and Paul's concern about exhibiting at all ('I don't see how you could ever show that anywhere') is not a difference of personality, bumptious ambition versus self-doubt, craven opportunism against steely integrity. It is a matter of the transformation of public taste and of the moral and aesthetic framework for the reception of images of war. Both artists are wrong, for cultural forces more powerful than the art schools or the avant-garde have promoted representations of the suffering of the Great War to the status of secular icons. The novel is replete with descriptions of the body in pain, but Barker is also alert to the wider cultural significance of representing wounds: within the series of depictions of the body remodelled by trauma in *Life Class* are two which mediate the shift from the Passion to the demotic pieta. The first is a rewriting of a long-standing Great War symbol, the roadside calvary:

a shattered crucifix stood in the middle of desolation, the figure of Christ reduced to one hand hanging from a nail. He hated that hand: it offended him that such a banal image should have so much power. (223)

Shrunk to little more than the stigmata, the figure is an all too obvious representation and representative of the soldiers who plead for the ambulance to stop. But these men have in a sense superseded Christ as the century's sacrificial victims, a status evinced by their stigmata:

They had no faces, only flaking mud masks with white circles round the eyes and red wet mouths struggling to speak. When words failed, they pointed to their wounds. (225)

The debate in *Life Class* about the role of art in wartime is constellated across the three parties to the novel's sexual triangle. Elinor's argument that it is business as usual at the Slade is contradicted by Tonks's reversion to medicine; Kit reveals unusual self-understanding in his realization that by making a career as a war artist he is 'chained to a historical event' (C. W. R. Nevinson's war saw him adopt an increasingly naturalist idiom, and he achieved notoriety by defying the rules of censorship, not those of painterly style). Paul's determination to exhibit is a symptom of artistic envy, a motive more powerful than either the obligation of the witness or conformity to the canons of taste, decency or privacy.

But there is a further dimension to the question of the recruitment of art to war. London is full of posters:

> One in particular pursued [Paul] from street to street. A jack-booted German officer trod on a dead woman's bare breasts, while behind them a village burnt. Beside the picture was a letter from a serving British soldier
>
> We have got three girls in the trenches with us, who came for protection. One has no clothes on, having been outraged by the Germans ... Another poor girl has just come in having had both her breasts cut off. Luckily I caught a Uhlan officer in the act and with a rifle shot at 300 yards killed him. And now she is with us but poor girl I am afraid she will die. She is very pretty and only about 19 and only has her skirt on. (237)

As Stuart Sillars has shown, the absence of journalistic photography meant that the work of illustrators was crucial to forming public knowledge about the critical events of the war (Sillars, passim). But Paul's reflex analysis of the 'cynicism' of this advertisement (using sex to sell war) should not be seen to quarantine painting from this potent genre of populist and propagandist iconography. After all, Paul understands intimately the power of such images: '[h]e guessed that glimpse of the girl with her skirt around her waist had frightened [Elinor] as much as it had aroused him' (126). There is a sense that the poster artist has made explicit something about war and art which Paul, in portraying what he saw, can only begin to hint at with his self-portrait as torturing-nurse. *Double Vision* is troubled by a comparable insight into the complicity with violence of both witness and audience, either when conscripted by mass media or when atrocity is contemplated without an outlet in action or moral decision.

We cannot resolve these problems by crediting Barker's own fiction of war as an adequate art of atrocity. For the most generous achievement in all of these novels is the relentless refraction of concepts through the specificity of dialogue and analogy. Barker's own representations of violence and war are immune neither from the charge that there are aspects of war she does not succeed in showing, nor from the claim that there are things she shows which she should not. But more than any contemporary writer on war, her work incarnates the commitment to transcend the partisan or the one-sided point of view.

PART III
Criticism and Contexts

7

CRITICAL RECEPTION

There are a number of ways of accounting for a writer's reception, for the way their work has been received, and one can begin by asking received by who? The word reception has several senses, which suggest the range of our potential concerns here: a theatrical ovation, acceptance or admittance ('into a place, company, state'), a radio signal getting through without interference. Indeed, one can construct a revealing history of literary studies according to the relative importance given to the way writing is received: for instance, Aristotle's theory of tragedy (fourth century BC) is very much concerned with the effects of performance on the audience, but by the time literary study had been established within Anglo-American universities in the mid-twentieth century, such talk had been outlawed as the 'affective fallacy', the error of confusing the verbal and formal properties of the literary work with its psychological effect on a reader. Indeed, the successful reception or admittance of English in the contest for authority among the modern university faculties can be identified with the dissemination of the formalist procedures of close reading or practical criticism. It can also be linked with broadly shared assumptions about which works were worth expending critical scrutiny upon. The name of F. R. Leavis, or of the journal, *Scrutiny*, he founded or of his study of the novel, *The Great Tradition* (1948), are often used as a shorthand for this confidence about the existence of a canon of literature, a class of works which had been received into the category of classic.

One could account for much of the recent turbulence in literary studies, since the rise of the discipline of English, in terms of questions such as how is the canon selected, how is it that canonical texts communicate across historically distinct cultures and what are the ideological functions of canonical literature? Thus feminists have challenged a predominantly patriarchal canon (though Leavis's 'great tradition' was founded by Jane Austen and George Eliot) which has systematically suppressed women's creativity, and the value of women's experience, by excluding women's writing from critical attention, refusing it a serious reception. Formalism – the assumption that the meaning of a work of literature is evident from its verbal and formal properties studied in isolation – has also been challenged by historical orientations, even in the development of reader-response theories of literature. Hans-Robert Jauss (1921–97), associated with the Constance School in Germany, asserted the importance of literary history in accounting for the generation of literary meaning, while Stanley Fish (1938–), in the United States, argued that meaning depended on the consent, and implicit assumptions, of an interpretive community. Theorists who, like Jerome McGann, emphasized the surprisingly easily overlooked facts of a literary work's material and economic embodiment – did you pay for the book in your hands, or did you borrow it from a library with a closed membership or are you reading it via some form of Internet piracy? – helped form a sub-discipline called the History of the Book which studies how the book as material object shapes verbal meaning. Meanwhile, politically oriented historicists, some of whom were inspired by a Marxian critique of ideology, were drawing attention to the way the canon, and associated institutions of literary education, operated to reproduce and defend vested political and economic interests (they might have pointed to the official report written in 1921 by Sir Henry Newbolt, famous for the line 'Play up, play up and play the game' ('Vitaï Lampada'), on the importance of the teaching of vernacular literature in English schools for nation building in the wake of the Great War).

The very fact that most of the readership of this book will use it as part of some accredited course of study is testament to changes in the literary canon, and hence in the patterns of reception of contemporary literature. While Barker is not canonical in the sense that John Milton is, her work is associated with that of canonical writers in some academic contexts (e.g., on the Assessment and Qualifications Alliance (AQA) synoptic paper on the literature of the Great War, which so many English A level students studied in the first decade of the twenty-first century) and is subject to a similar academic apparatus of peer-reviewed, footnoted articles in learned journals, student essays marked for their conformity to academic models by university professors, and nowadays, what some regard as the gold standard of academic reputation, the single-author monograph.

How Barker's work achieved this particular prominence – which by no means guarantees material and status rewards in the form of steady sales to 'captive' undergraduate readerships, collected editions or prizes for career achievement – could be investigated in institutional terms: how and why did contemporary literature come to challenge the classics, literature which has passed the 'test of time', in literary education? But more pertinently, in the present context, we can reflect on the forms and processes of selection which have given rise to Barker's status as a prestigious, significant or even representative contemporary novelists (the latter in the sense of exemplifying the aesthetic or thematic concerns of her age). We can also attend to the particular ways in which her work is understood, that is, how and in what ways her work is valued (a large majority of novels written are never published, and a large majority of novels published are not read a decade after publication). To do this, we can assemble a number of kinds of evidence, for instance reviews in the local, national and international press or academic assessments as well as set-book status on courses. These evaluations are, from one perspective, the opinions of informed individuals (they don't tell us what readers make of a novel but, as 'authoritative' judgements, they have significant influence on whether or not a novel gets read). From another point of view, they are elements in a mechanism that determines the winners and losers in a contest for sales and status which is not primarily a matter of judicious literary comparison (imagine what career-novelists feel about the commercial success of novels by famous gardening broadcasters or models).

The same argument can be applied with respect to, say, gender. It is no accident that when Pat Barker published her fiction with the avowedly feminist press Virago, as she did throughout the 1980s, her reviewers (i.e., the authorities appointed to assess her work in public by the editors of newspapers and journals) were predominantly female, and that her status as a novelist was marginal. This is not to impugn the authority of female reviewers – *Blow Your House Down* received notices written by the novelist Jane Rogers, the playwright Michelene Wandor, the sociologist Angela McRobbie and the editor Anne Boston – but to identify the way Barker's work was being placed before its potential audience. Where does reception start? Or indeed, is reception already in an important sense over by the time publishers and their agents of advertisement (e.g., the press, chat shows) have packaged a novel? The meanings of Barker's earlier fictions were over-determined, by her subject matter, by her publisher's reputation as a young firm with a political mission, and by the reinforcement of the 'women's novel' classification in the selection of reviewers.

Regeneration represents a turning point in all three respects. Barker's subject was now national and historical (why the subject of *The Century's Daughter* – the experience of working-class English women in the twentieth century – isn't easily recognizable as national and historical is another matter, reflected in the revised title, *Liza's England*). She had changed her publisher, and her work was now reviewed by men: the significance of a notice by Samuel Hynes, in the *New York Times Book Review*, was larger than his measured assessment of Barker's decision to regenerate the anti-war novel by telling a 'part of the whole story of war that is not often told' (Hynes). It lay also in Hynes being a celebrated East Coast academic and critic, a Second World War veteran aviator and the author of the recently published *A War Imagined* (1990), then the most important book on the literature of the Great War since Fussell's *The Great War and Modern Memory*. The association with Hynes's scholarship bolstered the associations Barker had created for herself by choosing to write about Sassoon and Owen (though fame and fortune have not – yet – greeted the authors of two other novels based on the lives of often-anthologized First World War poets, Geoff Akers's *Beating for Light: The Story of Isaac Rosenberg* (2005) and Robert Edric's narrative about Ivor Gurney, *In Zodiac Light* (2008)). Writing in the *Guardian*, the novelist Philip Hensher noted that *Regeneration* answered 'worrying questions ... about her range' (Westeman, 63).

Reviews are only one means by which the repute of a novelist is constructed and consolidated. In a predominantly visual era – TV, computer gaming, Video and DVD, cinema – the purchase of film rights and adaptations of novels into screenplays represent a significant economic prize in their own right, and can develop sales and celebrity through direct (tie-in editions) and indirect publicity. But cinematic 'adaptation' provides additional contexts for evaluating a writer's relationship to her own reception, because films are not just instances of high-profile attention, they are symptomatic readings or misreadings of the work. In the case of Pat Barker, the film industry's dependence on, and indifference to, literary material provides a case study of the way writing is read to conform with what Jauss called horizons of expectation, crudely put the ways in which we accommodate the disturbing or unexpected to the familiar and the normative.

Stanley and Iris (1990) is a romantic drama starring Jane Fonda (*Nine to Five*, and a Hollywood reputation for political activism) and Robert De Niro (*Raging Bull, Taxi Driver*). The screenplay was co-written by Harriet Frank Jr, and her husband Irving Ravetch: her previous cinema credit was co-writing *Hud*, the contemporary Western based on a Larry McMurty novel, starring Paul Newman, for which she was Oscar-nominated in 1963. Widowed, middle-class Iris meets proletarian Stanley at their workplace, in a bakery: their romance develops when he asks her to teach him to read. The film conforms to the generic cues of the made-for-TV thesis movie, the uplifting ending serving to confirm the possibility of realizing the social, moral and political goals for which the principal characters have had to struggle against popular or establishment indifference or opposition. Such films often deal with human experiences which the ideological norms of middle-class life in the United States determine are secrets (sexual abuse of children, or, in this case, illiteracy). If the film does anything surprising, it is throwing the talents of director Martin Ritt (*The Spy*

Who Came in From the Cold, 1965), Fonda and De Niro at a project so thin, and conventional, though Fonda was about to 'retire' from film to make fitness videos, and De Niro was 'cashing in' (Thomson, 224).

The reader can be forgiven for not recognizing the Barker novel adapted here: the film's credits indicate that it is based on *Union Street*, though it is still a challenge to recognize the narrative of Iris King and her daughter's pregnancy as the basis of the screenplay. The adaptation – namely the screenplay's lack of faithfulness to the textual property, its substitutions, suppressions and distractions – tells us more than any analysis of reviews about the gap between Barker's representation of women's experience of work and family in the 1980s and the images that even a socially progressive film could present. The family on the screen must be completed by a man (De Niro's Stanley), and the male's flaw, with its generational repetition, must be overcome. The socioeconomic relocation, whereby the character of the indominatable mother is promoted to the middle class, is in part a transatlantic translation; the transcendence of the family unit and its self-completion against the threats of the social mass are generic fixes to deal with Barker's disjunctive narrative and its troubling refusal to resolve life stories. *Stanley and Iris* represents the disappearance or even censoring of *Union Street*, and of Iris King, and a certain cultural illiteracy (two generations later, the genre of the recovery memoir, the story of abuse suffered, brought to light and overcome, would reconfigure the inadmissibility of poverty and domestic violence as 'literary' subject matter). The film confirms the cultural resistance to both the meanings and the forms of Barker's early work.

Gillies MacKinnon's film of *Regeneration* (1997) is an altogether more respectful treatment and its cast signalled, in Britain especially, reverence for a prestige literary property. The face of the actor James Wilby (Siegfried Sassoon) is strongly associated with the look of Merchant-Ivory films (a style of literary adaptation of twentieth-century classics such as E. M. Forster or Evelyn Waugh which became influential in the 1980s). But Barker's novel was not sufficiently well known for the details of the adaptation to be a focus of American reviews, which sought to locate *Regeneration* in relation to the war-movie, a genre whose essential ambivalence had been recently redefined by Stephen Spielberg's *Saving*

Private Ryan (1998; the US release of *Regeneration* was a month later in August 1998). Spielberg's high-budget reconstruction of the D-Day landings was widely held to have reinvented the aesthetics of the war film (particularly through its imagery of wounding, its sound and its editing), but MacKinnon's more domestic-scale treatment offered its own innovations in the depiction of battle (the opening tracking sequence solves the visual problem of the Western Front as battlefield by revealing the trenches from a few metres above, a visual homage to Owen's poem 'The Show'; Owen's proleptic tunnel nightmare, which opens into a *nature mort* on the Sambre canal, scene of his death). MacKinnon was caught between the expectations of the genre, that the adventure of combat be depicted (so we witness Mad Jack Sassoon's gung-ho offensiveness) and the insistence of the novel that the war's horrors are to be found in a mental hospital. MacKinnon's respectful reserve in this respect, together with the verbally overloaded screenplay, creates a problem of temporality, which illuminates Barker's skill in determining a form for her story. Barker uses repetition to prompt the reader to analogous thinking, primarily through the device of the psychoanalytic session. In the film the dialogue between doctor (Jonathan Pryce) and patients is dispersed throughout the hospital and its grounds, and across the diurnal regimen of meals, organized leisure, consultations and medical Boards, while intervals are accelerated to achieve a duration of just under 2 hours. Reaction shots underline Rivers's provocations to his patients, and Prior's antagonism to Rivers, but there is no cinematic device to elaborate paradox, as opposed to stating bald ironies: 'I'm getting shell-shocked by my patients.' More successful is the way Prior's ambivalence is brought out by Sarah Lumb, who views him as a toff ('don't you people have Christian names?') and who pointedly removes Billy's leather glove before putting his hand back on her breast. The novel's open-endedness is also a challenge, met partly by bringing forward Owen's death from the end of *The Ghost Road*, and by substituting the poet's words for Barker's, and Owen for Sassoon: Pryce's Rivers reassures Wilby's Sassoon that perhaps 'the protest of the old' will 'bring things to an end' (a disingenuous insistence on transference, as well as a dialogue derived from the novel's internalized free indirect discourse). The film ends with Rivers's tearful reading of Owen's 'Parable of the Old Man and the Young', a text introduced by screenwriter Allan Scott. The introduction of this bitter, allegorical rewriting of the Biblical story of Abraham and Isaac underlines what the film's faithfulness to Barker's words reveals about the writing of the novel, and the way it holds its issues in suspension.

Since the completion of the *Regeneration* trilogy, Barker's writing has become the subject of an increasingly sophisticated academic reception. It is now possible to discern the emergence of a community of scholars whose work is in dialogue over a number of recurrent issues (it requires a critical mass of literary critical interest to bring about a collective reassessment) and which is beginning to situate Barker's work in larger literary contexts. It is interesting that the dominant theme in this work, reflecting and in a sense reinforcing the resistance to the implications of Barker's earlier writing, is trauma (i.e., the psychological and literary registration of historical and somatic crisis). Thus Peter Childs describes Barker in her own words as a writer 'in the shadow of monstrosities' and reads the working-class novels as preliminaries to a 'fuller understanding' of violence and its representation (Childs, 69, 78).

Ian Haywood, in a discussion of 'Post-Industrial Fictions', relates Barker's early novels to 'the postwar Left's blindness to issues of gender' (Haywood, 144). Paulina Palmer had linked Barker with Margaret Atwood, in 'treating violence as *the* distinguishing feature of a male supremacist society' (Palmer, 88). In *Dialogics of the Oppressed*, Peter Hitchcock develops the ideas of Bakhtin to argue that Barker heads off the extinction of the working-class novel with dialogic devices. According to Hitchcock, Barker avoids the pitfalls of reification identified by Dodds and Dodds through a radical writing which 'is a refraction more than a reflection of existence in sign' (Hitchcock, 1993, 56). Other scholars have linked issues of gender and class to the emerging historical and memorial themes in Barker's writing. John Kirk's 'Recovered Perspectives' (1999) argues that the 'act of remembering comes to be seen as a radical act in itself' (624). In 'Compulsory Masculinity' (1998), Greg Harris addresses homosexuality and masculine codes in the trilogy, a question taken up with greater insistence on class politics by Hitchcock in 'What Is Prior?' (2002).

Critical Perspectives on Pat Barker (2005), a substantial overview of her fiction up to *Double Vision*, marked the formal identification of an international group of Barker scholars as well as the fact that the novelist's work no longer required advocacy, and that critical analysis of it no longer required apology. The volume also printed playwright Sarah Daniels' stage version of *Blow Your House Down*, another adaptation of Barker's writing which reveals just how incendiary and discomforting her treatment of violence can be (the rape and murder of Kath is substituted by the figure of the 'Chicken Man'). The assembled critics are concerned both to reassess and to contextualize. John Brannigan reads *Union Street* in relation to British fiction about working-class women, and furthermore as 'demythologizing homelessness' (Monteith et al., 2005, 4). Similarly, Sharon Monteith seeks historical cinematic correlatives for the fantasy screenplay which reveals the gaps in 'compulsory masculinity' in *The Man Who Wasn't There* (121). Ronald Paul compares Barker's 'female view of the war' with the 'naturalist, semi-documentary' classics of war fiction by Barbusse, Hemingway and Remarque in order to show how her work counters pastoral tendencies in the literary memorialization of the Great War with an insistence on social, and class, contexts of war experience. Dennis Brown analyzes the trilogy as a 'tour de force of well-researched intertextuality' (188).

Brannigan's book on Barker, published in the same year, was the first full-length study of her work by a single author (Karin Westeman's short book on *Regeneration* appeared in 2001). Brannigan gives equal emphasis to all stages of Barker's career, and thus corrects a tendency to downplay the importance of the earlier fiction in developmental readings of her oeuvre. He argues for the experimental character of her writing, in comparison with more famous contemporaries like Amis and McEwan included in *Granta's* 'Young British Novelists' project, as a 'critique of class and gender politics' achieved by 'adapting and subverting conservative narrative forms' (Brannigan, 2005, 37).

The convergence between Barker's career and the intersections between psychoanalysis, medicine and literature, which led to the formation of 'Trauma Theory' as an explicit orientation in the humanities since the 1990s, has shaped recent scholarship. Ankhi Mukherjee's 'Stammering to Story' imaginatively links the fictional Rivers's concept of the stammer as conflict between speech and self-censorship to the profusion of symptoms and transferences in Barker's writing. Kenneth Pellew's 'Analogy in

Regeneration' offers similarly illuminating analyses of the forms of Barker's writing without the psychoanalytic terminology, noting how every dialogue 'contains and reflects every other' (145). Trauma, and its representation, is also the focus of the work on Barker by Anne Whitehead, who contributed a highly informative essay on psychotherapy and history to *Critical Perspectives*. Her 'The Past as Revenant' (2004) reads *Another World* as a novel which makes the dissociation at the core of trauma a lever for opening up the novel's historically and thematically dissociated materials, notably war and infanticide.

The psychoanalytic community itself is responsible for the most intriguing encounter with Barker in interview. Her exchanges with Catherine Garland, the most charged of a sequence of innovative pairings of novelists with psychologists convened in Leicester in 2003 by Arabella Kurtz, were published in the journal *Psychology and Psychotherapy* (2004). Barker's writing is a sustained dialogue, not with the therapeutic community, but about the ambivalence of therapeutic goals in a century characterized by its sensitivity *and* indifference to trauma. Her novels have persistently challenged theoretical generalizations about the significance of traces of violence in memory, but have also come to weigh seriously the role of art and literature in shaping our consciousness of war.

8

AUTHOR INTERVIEW

MR Can I begin by asking you about *Life Class* and its relationship to *Regeneration*: what I'd like to explore is why and how you returned to the terrain of the First World War.

PB I suppose I was given quite a few hints by my agent, that it would be a good thing to do professionally. Also I felt I'd had a 10-year gap and I had different things to say. I think there was only one passage in *Life Class* where I felt that I was tending to repeat in a way that I didn't want to do, and that was where Paul was looking at the landscape around Ypres. That landscape is so dominant in memories and representations of the war, and it has also come to stand in for all war. An alarm bell rang.

MR Arguably, some of the richest dialogues in your work occur when you return to a situation or theme, and take another look at it.

PB What I was exploring, and may explore further in future, is that what happened to the body, the male body, was unshowable, and that in fact the landscape stands in for the body. Tonks's pastel portraits are really the only totally realistic representation of what happened to the body, yet Tonks himself said that the significant art that came out of the war would be landscape painting. He too believed that the way to the truth about what happened to people was to show what happened to the landscape.

MR *Regeneration* emphasized the mental wounds.

PB But of course the war neuroses are physical. There is Burns who incessantly vomits and becomes emaciated, and in *The Ghost Road* there is the extraordinary Moffet – they unrolled his paralysis down his legs like a pair of surgical stockings and he couldn't stop it happening. So there is the sense in which hysteria is the body language of protest, but in *Life Class* you are starting with physical injuries to which the emotional trauma would be secondary. One of the things that interests me is the extent to which the wound becomes a way of not dealing with the mental trauma. In the case of facially injured men, who have become unrecognizable to themselves, it is not possible that they didn't suffer trauma, yet you don't get the impression people were thinking about that at all.

MR Trauma has become a prominent theme in the academic humanities in recent years; was there any sense in which your return to the First World War was a corrective to this emphasis in the academic reading of your own work?

PB No I didn't think of it as a rethinking. I didn't think very much about the relationship between the *Regeneration* trilogy and *Life Class*, except that I wanted it to be different in as many ways as possible. One of the other differences of course is that there is not the dominant older figure that you have in Rivers, nor apart from Tonks is there any real use of a named historical figure. That changes the tone of the book, the fact that all the protagonists are quite young, the oldest would be 25 or 26. What fascinated me was the before and after, the hinge on which their whole experience of life turned, and how much more dramatic that is when you've got young people of 20, 21, 22, which is the age of maximum choice.

MR That metaphor of a hinge between worlds has been a recurrent image of the First World War since 1914.

PB It is a sort of solstice, and the solstice is traditionally the time when very strange things are allowed to enter the world. At least in the autumn solstice. That's when the ghosts get in.

MR Ghosts have just got into our conversation. I'm curious about that.

PB Ghosts as metaphors for whatever in the past we haven't managed to resolve. I'm not a great believer in the supernatural. Strangely, having been brought up by spiritualists I think I am about the most insensitive person I know where that kind of thing is concerned. I could sit in Borley Rectory and have a good night's sleep and I'm sure not see a thing. I'm sure other people did.

MR Back in the 1960s, Ted Hughes called the First World War the 'national ghost'.

PB It is not so much the national ghost as the Matter of Britain, even more so than Arthur and his Knights. It is only when you go to other countries, including some which were more embroiled in the war, that you realize that we see it in a quite specific way.

MR *Life Class* shifts the hinge from the military to the personal.

PB I also displaced it to 1914, whereas conventionally it is 1916, with conscription, rather than the Somme. That was why I needed my characters to be not fit to serve. Paradoxically, Neville and Tarrant get to the Front in record time precisely because the Army rejects them. If they'd joined the Army, the very earliest they could have been in France would have been May 1915. As it is, they were there in late September, October, and experiencing that first absolutely catastrophic battle where the French lost a quarter of a million dead in no time at all.

MR Is this another way of writing away from the dominant myths of the Great War, getting in, as it were, before they have established themselves?

PB Yes, I think it is. I think writing about ambulance men and orderlies is another way. But there are so many dominant myths. Another is the war poet who is a sensitive officer, who suffered trauma, and there's a contrary myth that ordinary private soldiers managed perfectly well. Most of the mental casualties were private soldiers, but they were sent to Maghull Hospital.

MR Are these medical or literary myths?

PB No, I think it is a historical myth. There is a point of view that it was a perfectly reasonable war to fight, and that the critique of the war as pointless slaughter is wrong. What can you say? Somebody says this is worth eight million dead: the only possible reply to that is no it isn't.

MR Is that the role of narrative fiction in relation to this Matter of Britain?

PB All the novelist ever contributes is a sense of the complexity of the issues as they are worked out in individual lives. The novelist has a boring role of saying neither the issues nor the feelings are as simple as they appear. I really see the novelist as the opposite of the missionary or the proselytizer of any kind. We are the great sayers of 'yes, but . . . .'

MR Boring? Because this work of negation must be done again and again?

PB The worth of fiction has to be asserted over and over again. It is the only form that makes you think deeply and feel strongly, not as alternative modes of reaction, but as part of a single, unified reaction. There is nothing else that does that. In other kinds of writing either one reaction or the other is preferred, and generally it is the thinking clearly and deeply which is preferred. Historians and sociologists deal in generalizations about people, rightly so, and it is only the novelist who insists on the unique and recalcitrant and atypical human being who is quite often swimming, not very heroically, or self-consciously, against the stream. And it is celebrating that individual that is really what novelists are about.

MR I'm particularly interested in the ways in which your oeuvre might be said to be in dispute with itself, returning to scenarios or contradictions and particularizing them in a different way. For example, Muriel Scaife's nursing of her husband in *Union Street* is transformed into Stephen's care for his father in *Liza's England*.

PB I see a contrast, rather than a resemblance. Muriel is doing something creative, helping the child to grieve for his father, and saving him from being an unpleasant little jerk. I was interested in people being creative with life, rather than art, in their dealings with other people – you can be either creative or destructive – and Muriel is extraordinarily creative. In *Union Street* I was aware of writing about people not given much credit for what they do, which can be not far short of heroic. Stephen I see as being much less creative, much more a recipient of others' creativity.

MR I've always been struck by the substitution, the situation is identical but angled so differently.

PB My first draft of the death of the father in *Union Street* was done from the boy's point of view but this unbalanced the novel, and I rewrote it from Muriel's point of view. So in *Liza's England* it is restored to what I originally felt like doing, which is an episode between the father and the son. I did once have somebody point out the repetition to me. It is quite horrific, the vomiting of blood – I did actually witness it twice – so my answer was if it happens to me twice I'm justified in using it twice.

MR In *Union Street* you work in facets, seven episodes which are also a concept of how the lives relate to each other as seven ages. How did you arrive at that arc, and its articulation?

PB The characters actually share memories; one character will remember something that happened to another. There is a sense, a rather timid sense, that it is not quite seven different women; it is a little bit more complicated than that. But I don't think I was bold enough to take it all the way to having a rather extraordinary central character, who is almost a cubist portrait of a single person. In a sense there is only one woman in *Union Street*. One of the reasons I wrote *Liza's England* was that I wanted to take a woman and pay her the compliment of actually doing a full-length portrait of her. But in many ways I think *Union Street* was a more interesting structure. And *Blow Your House Down* comes out of *Union Street*, because although I rewrote the Muriel Scaife episode, of course in Blonde Dinah, although she is a central character, you do actually see her from the man's point of view. I felt slightly uneasy about that, she was called Fair Lill in real life. *Blow Your House Down* was an apology to Blonde Dinah for not giving her her own point of view on the events of her life and death. There is a movement from one book to the next; it is not generally a matter of returning over several books.

MR Are we invited to think of Danny and Peter as a serial character?

PB They are more or less the same person. But it wasn't a big enough character to take that, not enough complexity. What I would like to do, if I was to do anything with him, is make him into a psychotherapist, so you come full circle. There's no reason why he couldn't be, he could take a counseling course, and he would get through on his surface social skills. There's little regulation of the counseling industry. And he would want to do it, for all the wrong reasons.

MR Are there connections between his ambition to get inside people's heads as a therapist, and the qualities you give to his short stories, qualities which raise interesting issues about readers' identifications with fiction?

PB It's because there is no identity, he can only cling-film himself round other people to give himself a shape. One of the archetypal figures is the figure of the shape-shifter, the person who can transform themselves endlessly. Something that witches were supposed to be able to do. The terror of that fascinates me, because it is the terror of unknowability and unreliability, rather than any more obvious aggressive or hostile characteristics. What interests me is the relationship to Billy Prior. Peter is much more negative than Billy. There is a moment midway through the trilogy when Rivers can no longer take Prior's insinuations, and makes him change places, and he is making Prior confront the responsibilities of what he undertakes to do. But Danny wouldn't see that there were any responsibilities. I'm not sure I fully understand what River's changing places means; it is like Burns taking his clothes off and arranging the dead animals around him. If it could be explained in other terms it wouldn't need to happen. I think Rivers at that point feels genuinely challenged, and he does a creative thing. About all he has left he can do.

MR I want to ask you about the writing process in relation to what we now call the *Regeneration* trilogy. I'm uncertain as to what I've understood about the genesis of the novels from other interviews you have given.

PB Part of responding to the person is not being consistent.

MR Did you decide to write *The Eye in the Door* because *Regeneration* had worked, because it had produced lots of fruitful contradictions?

PB I certainly felt the story wasn't finished at the end of *Regeneration*, because I tried to give it a sense of completion but of course you can't, because Rivers is in a state of deeper conflict at the end of the book than he is at the beginning, and Sassoon is going back to the war which he still opposes as much as he ever did. Neither of those characters have a position of rest. Oddly enough, Prior is in more of a resting position at the end of *Regeneration* because he has been placed on permanent home service. I tried to give *Regeneration* a sense of cohesion and then I rewrote it to make it seem deliberately incomplete. With the beginning of *The Eye in the Door* I went round and round in circles for a long time. I knew I wanted a character whose internal division would mirror all the divisions of the war: before and after; Home Front and front line; the Germans, us and no man's land in the middle. I wanted a character whose own dissociation would mimic that division. Then I realized I already had a dissociated character, ostensibly cured, and I also remembered that he had been great fun to write about.

MR And the hinge between *The Eye in the Door* and *The Ghost Road*?

PB Once again, the fear of repetition. I knew I had to get Rivers out from behind his desk. I had done everything I could do with the conflicted therapist. And of course Rivers had made the choice not to be a conflicted therapist; he was only a therapist during the war. I decided there had to be the flashback to Rivers the anthropologist, which is what Rivers had chosen to be, despite his training as a neurologist. And then you had this wonderful thing, to me, of a society which was very much a warrior community.

MR The structure of *The Ghost Road*, which parallels anthropological researches with the experiment of sending Prior back, is different to the more multiply-faceted form of the other two novels. This gives the parallel between the suppressed warrior culture in the Pacific with the disguised warrior culture in Europe a tremendous inevitability. Was this a discovery resulting from moving Rivers back into the world of his own choices?

PB I was also interested in what so many people said, that the world didn't change in 1916, it had changed in 1910. Virginia Woolf says it, Lytton Strachey says it, Rivers also says it. In the visual arts too, [Roger Fry's] exhibition of 1910, and Tonks saying 'don't go'. It was a time of great ferment. Christopher Nevinson said that artists had been at war since 1910, and this was unmistakably true for him; this is when he started to paint in the futurist manner more or less. The moment for Rivers was having his questions turned back on him by Pacific islanders, and he saw himself through their eyes, and saw the validity of what they were looking at, and how peculiar it was in their terms. That was the moment of change. He mentions it more than once; it was obviously a matter of some significance to him.

MR Your fiction represents big ideas as the implications of concrete occurrences and this is a good example, where we recognize the analogy between the therapeutic encounter and 'cross-cultural recognition'. How do you keep so many ideas in play, without them becoming abstractions?

PB   There are two sorts of writer. One writer knows what the character ought to do, and sets out to persuade the reader. The other writer doesn't know what the character ought to do because it is a genuinely difficult dilemma. I feel strongly you've got to put yourself on the line; if you know the answer, you shouldn't be asking the question. Somebody said to me, was Rivers right or was Sassoon right? What a question! Who knows? It is also a technical matter. It is very easy to tell the story in your particular voice as a writer, and tell the reader what to think. But as soon as you start to dramatize, as soon as you want the characters to speak, that is incredibly revealing. If you dramatize, you are putting yourself on the line in a way you are not if you are telling a story, simply narrating.

It is very important not to know what the answers to the characters' dilemmas are. You may think by the end of the book that you have discovered it, but it must be a process of investigation and inquiry; it is not a matter of deciding what you think about something and then writing fiction to illustrate what you think. The fiction is the thinking.

MR   I have a sense of you as a novelist who returns to certain questions in strikingly different ways . . .

PB   It probably means I still don't know the answer, and if I don't come back I suppose that means that matter has been sorted out in some way for me.

MR   Can I get you to say something about how *Double Vision* and *Life Class* are deliberate reflections on questions of representing violence.

PB   *Life Class* belongs with *Double Vision* rather than the trilogy. I saw them as twin books. I suppose I really think *Life Class* is a stronger discussion of the subject, though some people prefer the contemporary relevance of *Double Vision*. It is strange, the way I have described Paul's painting of the front – the landscapes, which are obviously rather like Paul Nash – it is largely a corpse-free zone, but so of course in television reporting of Afghanistan and Iraq. That was what links the novels, Paul Nash. I'm not at all sure that that wasn't the moment that I made up my mind to go back. I was aware all the time in writing *Double Vision* – talking about Ben's photographs, and about Goya and his Disasters of War series which he never allowed to be shown in his lifetime – of Nash and Nevinson and the artists of the First World War, and that these same issues could be discussed in those terms as well. I think *Double Vision* led me back. Which is why I get slightly uneasy when people ask why did I return to the world of the trilogy. I didn't, I wrote *Double Vision* and moved on. I think every one of my books comes quite directly from the one before it. It might not be apparent what the connections are, but I am sure they are there.

MR   Having thought about your work as an oeuvre, could we talk about the categories your writing has been placed into? Being a Virago author, for instance?

PB   *Union Street* and Virago were a brilliant fit. I got increasingly impatient with the Northern working-class, gritty, feminist label, and I got fed up answering the question why do you never write about men? I felt it was a straight-jacket in terms of the subjects I could deal with. Virago would have said they could have published *Regeneration*, but I don't think they could have, not in the way Penguin did. *The Man Who Wasn't There* was a kind of transitional book, a Virago hardback and a Penguin paperback. You move out of one slot into another slot, and I very rapidly became the First World War novelist, not with *Regeneration*, which got comparatively little attention, but as the trilogy moved on. I objected to that least. People started asking me, why don't you write about women? *Another World*, *Double Vision* and *Border Crossing* weren't particularly categorized. Everyone reacts against type-casting and it is just as destructive to react against it as to follow it. If you have a pot of gold, something you understand and can write about, you are bound to be type-cast on the basis of it, but you never like it.

MR   *Regeneration* has become part of a canon of English war writing.

PB   That is a continuing dilemma. Sassoon hated war but it gave him his voice. The war made Sassoon and broke him. Most people who write about war hate it but are nonetheless remembered for it.

MR   That coupling you suggested of being made and unmade by war is not reflected by the way we understand the literary culture of war, with its emphasis on the idea that writers are made by war. Something similar has been suggested about your writing, that war launched you as a writer.

PB Yes, I don't think war was the launching of my talent, but certainly the career. I started writing about things the literary establishment could understand, instead of all these awful women in the back streets of Middlesbrough. Not everyone sees that the writer is the same in both sets of books. A lot of the characters, and the attitudes and the dilemmas are the same as well. Of the three books in the trilogy, the least read is the most radical, *The Eye in the Door*, the one least connected with the battlefields.

MR What is involved in joining in the production, and reproduction, of a national discourse about the First World War?

PB The poets were a problem because they already had there own myth. So you were writing the legend, and having to write against it. Very few people knew about Rivers.

MR They do now.

PB He was easy, there were lots of gaps to fill in. Prior was not pure invention, no literary character is.

MR Prior and Owen converge.

PB Yes, they are mirror images, they are twins. A lot of what happens to Prior happened in a different form to Owen. Prior's sexual humiliation of the fawning older man is a variant of the claim that Owen was seduced or assaulted by a member of Robert Ross's set. They go back together, fight together, they die almost to the same minute, because that's the logic of their being fictional doubles.

One of the reasons it is a good thing to write historical novels is that it enables you to focus on the biological constants of human nature in a way that the contemporary novel never can. If you are going to keep the reader awake they have to identify with the character, but if it is a historical character all kinds of things will be different and alien so you have to go for the basic biological drives of human nature. You have to get all the other stuff right of course, but the other stuff is not what it is all about.

MR What kind of subject matter is war now?

PB There's an awful lot of it going on. Sixty-five million dead since 1945 from war. What are we as a species doing to each other? All the villages in the Yorkshire dales have their Great War memorial, usually with several names from one or two families; in other words brothers dying, and then crammed into a tiny space at the bottom are the Second War dead, there is no room for them because the earlier war was the War to End Wars, it was not going to happen again. Now the Armed Forces Memorial that was dedicated recently to the dead in the wars since 1945 has an immense space left for future names. The spaces are left to be filled and that is where we are.

MR I detect a sense that war stopped in 1945 as far as our culture is concerned.

PB It stopped as far as volunteers and conscripts are concerned.

MR Is that why recreation, imagining Britain's historical wars again, remains important?

PB It desanitizes war; it brings it home what it would have been like to be part of war, rather than seeing it as the fifth item on the news. The First World War doesn't really vanish with the veterans. It is not the veterans that the young people identify with, it is the young people who actually died. So I think it is a more durable thing than people sometimes allow for; they were the great lost generation sacrificed to the stupidity of their elders which is exactly what every generation of youth thinks is happening to it, so there is no reason for that identification to ever break down.

MR In *Another World* you juxtapose different ways of cultivating an interest in the past.

PB A lot of that sprang from a television programme I did after *The Ghost Road* where I was asked to interview a 103-year-old veteran, and the producer had her story board – it is never an open-ended interview – and she wanted me to ask him about war comradeship, and homoeroticism, and how it felt to kill people. I wasn't going to ask him about any of those things. We had taken him back to France and posed him looking down into a trench and I asked him, when you did that what did you think? And he said the exact opposite of what the producer wanted, he said he remembered how lonely we all were, it was so lonely. He had been a runner, which is maybe why he survived the 4 years of the war. He had a trade to return to, he was a printer, he had a girl and a family, and he served on the ack-ack guns in the Second World War and had a complete nervous breakdown which had obviously been waiting in the wings since he had been in the trenches. His nerves were perfect while he was out there, but in 1940 he was a wreck.

Geordie was based partly on my husband's father, who broke down. He had two delusions, that he had witnessed the bayoneting of his brother in France (which he had not), it was re-enacted before his eyes, and at a later stage he became convinced that his wife was the German soldier who had killed his brother so he kept attacking her. It was so poignant that here were two old people, in a kitchen in New York, fighting an episode from the battle of the Somme. It was amazing that that had happened. More than anything else, the feeling of it rising to the surface again, as repression weakens with age. I have spoken to so many people over the years; the audience have fed back into the books. There was one old lady whose older brothers had both been killed in the war. Their portraits hung in the hall when she was a little girl. For some reason women were forbidden to use the downstairs loo; that was for the men. One day she came in from the garden and in a spirit of great defiance she peed in the downstairs loo, and she came out into the hall, looked at these portraits, stamped her foot and said 'it wasn't my fault'. That is amazing, the guilt, the shadow.

BIBLIOGRAPHY

Ardis, Ann. 'Political Attentiveness vs. Political Correctness: Teaching Pat Barker's *Blow Your House Down*', in Sharon Monteith, Margaretta Jolly, Nahem Yousaf and Ronald Paul, eds, *Critical Perspectives on Pat Barker*. Columbia, SC: University of South Carolina Press, 2005: 14–23.

Bakhtin, Mikhail. *Problems of Dostoyevsky's Poetics*. Trans. Caryl Emerson. Manchester: Manchester University Press, 1984.

Barker, Pat. *Union Street*. London: Virago, 1982. Reprinted 2000.

———. *Blow Your House Down*. London: Virago, 1984. Reprinted 1995.

———. *Liza's England*. Formerly published as *The Century's Daughter*. London: Virago, 1986. Reprinted 1996.

———. *The Man Who Wasn't There*. London: Virago, 1989.

———. *Regeneration*. London: Vintage, 1991.

———. *The Eye in the Door*. London: Vintage, 1993.

———. *The Ghost Road*. London: Vintage, 1995.

———. *Another World*. London: Vintage, 1998.

———. *Border Crossing*. London: Vintage, 2001.

———. *Double Vision*. London: Hamish Hamilton, 2003.

———. *Life Class*. London: Hamish Hamilton, 2007.

Bartleet, Carina. 'Bringing the House Down: Pat Barker, Sarah Daniels, and the Dramatic Dialogue', in Sharon Monteith, Margaretta Jolly, Nahem Yousaf and Ronald Paul, eds, *Critical Perspectives on Pat Barker*. Columbia, SC: University of South Carolina Press, 2005: 87–100.

Baudrillard, Jean. *The Gulf War Did Not Take Place*. Sydney: Power Publications, 1995.

Brannigan, John. 'Pat Barker's *Regeneration* Trilogy: History and the Hauntological Imagination', in Richard Lane, Rod Mengham and Philip Tew, eds, *Contemporary British Fiction*. Cambridge: Polity Press, 2002: 13–25.

———. 'Interview with Pat Barker', *Contemporary Literature*, 46, 3 (2005): 367–392.

———. *Pat Barker*. Manchester: Manchester University Press, 2005.

Brearton, Fran. *The Great War in Irish Poetry: W.B. Yeats to Michael Longley*. Oxford: The Clarendon Press, 2000.

———. 'A War of Friendship: Robert Graves and Siegfried Sassoon', in Tim Kendall, ed., *Oxford Handbook of British and Irish War Poetry*. Oxford: Oxford University Press, 2007: 208–226.

Caesar, Adrian. *Taking It Like a Man: Suffering, Sexuality and the War Poets: Brooke, Sassoon, Owen, Graves.* Manchester: Manchester University Press, 1993.

Carter, Angela, *The Sadeian Woman.* London: Virago, 1979.

Caruth, Cathy. *Unclaimed Experience: Trauma, Narrative and History.* Baltimore, MD: Johns Hopkins University Press, 1996.

Cavell, Stanley. *The World Viewed: Reflections on the Ontology of Film.* Enlarged edition. Cambridge, MA: Harvard University Press, 1979.

Childs, Peter. *Contemporary Novelists.* London: Palgrave Macmillan, 2005.

Coleridge, S. T. *Biographia Literaria,* 2 vols. Oxford: The Clarendon Press, 1907.

Connelly, Mark. *We Can Take It!: Britain and the Memory of the Second World War.* London: Longman, 2004.

Davies, Martin. *Historics: Why History Dominates Contemporary Society.* London: Routledge, 2006.

Dawson, Graham. *Soldier Heroes: British Adventure, Empire and the Imagining of Masculinities.* London: Routledge, 1994.

De Quincey, Thomas. *The Works of Thomas de Quincey,* 21 vols. Ed. Grevel Lindop. London: Pickering and Chatto, 2000–2003.

Dodd, Kathryn and Dodd, Philip. 'From the East End to *EastEnders*: Representations of the Working Class, 1890–1990', in Dominic Strinati and Stephen Wagg, eds, *Come on Down? Popular Media Culture in Post-War Britain.* London: Routledge, 1992: 116–132.

Douglas, Keith. *The Complete Poems of Keith Douglas.* Ed. Desmond Graham. Oxford: Oxford University Press, 1978.

Duckworth, Alistair. 'Two Borrowings in Pat Barker's *Regeneration*', *Journal of Modern Literature*, 27, 3 (Winter 2004): 63–68.

Dyer, Geoff. *The Missing of the Somme.* London: Hamish Hamilton, 1994.

Dylan, Bob. *Highway 61 Revisited.* Columbia, 1965.

Eisenstein, Elizabeth. *The Printing Revolution in Early Modern Europe.* Cambridge: Cambridge University Press, 1993.

Eksteins, Modris. *Rites of Spring: The Great War and the Birth of the Modern Age.* London: Bantam, 1989.

Eliot, George. *Middlemarch.* Harmondsworth: Penguin, 1994.

———. *Adam Bede.* Oxford: Oxford University Press, 2008.

Ford, Ford Madox. *The English Novel: From the Earliest Days to the Death of Joseph Conrad.* Manchester: Carcanet, 1983.

Furedi, Frank. *Therapy Culture: Cultivating Vulnerability in an Uncertain Age.* London: Routledge, 2004.

Garland, Catherine. 'Conversation between Pat Barker and Catherine Garland', *Psychology and Psychotherapy: Theory, Research and Practice*, 77 (2004): 185–199.

Gilroy, Paul. *Between Camps: Nations, Culture and the Allure of Race.* London: Allen Lane, 2000.

Goya, *The Complete Etchings of Goya*. New York: Crown Publishers, 1943.

Gunby, Ingrid. *Postwar Englishness in the Fiction of Pat Barker, Graham Swift and Adam Thorpe*. Unpublished Ph.D. Thesis. University of Leeds, 2002.

Hacking, Ian. *Rewriting the Soul: Multiple Personality and the Sciences of Memory*. Princeton, NJ: Princeton University Press, 1995.

———. *The Social Construction of What?* Cambridge, MA: Harvard University Press, 2000.

Hamilton, Patrick. *The Slaves of Solitude*. Oxford: Oxford University Press, 1982.

Hanley, Lynsey. *Estates: An Intimate History*. London: Granta, 2008.

Harris, Greg. 'Compulsory Masculinity, Britain, and the Great War: The Literary-Historical Work of Pat Barker', *Studies in Contemporary Fiction*, 39, 4 (Summer 1998): 290–304.

Harrison, Mark. *Medicine and Victory: British Military Medicine in the Second World War*. Oxford: Oxford University Press, 2004.

Harrison, Tony. *Selected Poems*. Harmondsworth: Penguin, 1984.

Haywood, Ian. *Working-Class Fiction: From Chartism to* Trainspotting. London: Northcote House and the British Council, 1997.

Heaney, Seamus. *The Government of the Tongue*. London: Faber, 1988.

Hibberd, Dominic. *Wilfred Owen: A New Biography*. London: Weidenfeld & Nicolson, 2002.

Hitchcock, Peter. *Dialogics of the Oppressed*. Minneapolis: University of Minnesota Press, 1993.

———. 'What Is Prior?: Working-class Masculinity in Pat Barker's Trilogy', *Genders*, 35 (2002). Online journal located at http://www.genders.org, accessed 20 July 2009.

Hobsbawm, Eric. *Age of Empire*. London: Abacus, 1989.

Hughes, Ted. *Winter Pollen: Occasional Prose*. Ed. William Scammel. London: Faber, 1994.

Huxley, Aldous. *Crome Yellow*. Harmondsworth: Penguin, 1955.

Hyman, Timothy and Wright, Patrick, eds. *Stanley Spencer*. London: Tate Publishing, 2001.

Hynes, Samuel. *A War Imagined: The First World War and English Culture*. London: The Bodley Head, 1990.

———. 'Among Damaged Men', Review of *Regeneration*. *The New York Times Book Review* (29 March 1992): 1.

Itzin, Catherine, ed. *Pornography: Women, Violence and Civil Liberties: A Radical New View*. Oxford: Oxford University Press, 1992.

James, Henry. *The Turn of the Screw*, 2nd edn. Ed. Deborah Esch and Jonathan Warren. New York: Norton, 1999.

Jenkins, Phillip. *Using Murder: The Social Construction of Serial Homicide*. New York: Aldine de Gruyter, 1994.

Joannou, Maroula. 'Pat Barker and the Languages of Region and Class', in Emma Parker, ed., *Contemporary British Women Writers (Essays and Studies 2004)*. London: D.S. Brewer, 2005: 41–54.

Jouve, Nicole Ward. *'The Streetcleaner': The Yorkshire Ripper Case on Trial*. London: Marion Boyars, 1986.

Kirk, John. 'Recovered Perspectives: Gender, Class, and Memory in Pat Barker's Writing', *Contemporary Literature*, 40, 4 (1999): 603–625.

Larkin, Philip. *Required Writing: Miscellaneous Pieces 1955–1982*. London: Faber, 1983.

Lewis, Adrian R. *The American Culture of War: The History of U.S. Military Force from World War II to Operation Iraqi Freedom*. London: Routledge, 2007.

Lively, Penelope. *Moon Tiger*. Harmondsworth: Penguin, 1988.

Lukacs, Georg. *Writer and Critic*. London: Merlin, 1970.

MacDonald, Stephen. *Not About Heroes: The Friendship of Siegfried Sassoon and Wilfred Owen*. New York: Samuel French, 1987.

McCullin, Don. 'A Life in Photographs', *Granta*, 14 (1984): 171–196.

McEwan, Ian. *Enduring Love*. London: Jonathan Cape, 1997.

McNally, Richard J. *Remembering Trauma*. Cambridge, MA: Harvard University Press, 2003.

McRobbie, Angela. 'Cross Winds', review of Pat Barker, *Blow Your House Down*. *New Statesman* (8 June 1984): 25.

Micale, Mark S. and Lerner, Paul Frederick, eds. *Traumatic Pasts: History, Psychiatry and Trauma in the Modern Age, 1870–1930*. Cambridge: Cambridge University Press, 2001.

Monteith, Sharon. 'Pat Barker', in Sharon Monteith, Jenny Newman and Pat Wheeler, eds, *Contemporary British and Irish Fiction: An Introduction Through Interviews*. London: Arnold, 2004: 20–35.

Monteith, Sharon, Margaretta Jolly, Nahem Yousaf and Ronald Paul, eds. *Critical Perspectives on Pat Barker*. Columbia, SC: University of South Carolina Press, 2005.

Moretti, Franco. 'The Novel: History and Theory'. *New Left Review*, n.s. 52 (July/August 2008): 111–124.

Morrison, Blake. 'The Ballad of the Yorkshire Ripper', *London Review of Books* (4 July 1985): 9–10.

———. *Too True*. London: Granta, 1998.

Mukherjee, Ankhi. 'Stammering to Story: Neurosis and Narration in Pat Barker's *Regeneration*', *Studies in Contemporary Fiction*, 43, 1 (Fall 2001): 49–62.

Nietzsche, Friedrich. *The Birth of Tragedy*. New York: Dover, 1995.

———. *Beyond Good and Evil*. Ed. and Trans. R. J. Hollingdale. Harmondsworth: Penguin, 1973.

Nixon, Robert. 'An Interview with Pat Barker', *Contemporary Literature*, 45, 1 (2004): 1–21.

Nora, Pierre. 'Between Memory and History: *Les Lieux de Mémoire*', *Representations*, 26 (Spring 1989): 7–24.

Orwell, George. *Nineteen Eighty-Four*. Harmondsworth: Penguin, 1977.

Owen, Wilfred. *Selected Letters of Wilfred Owen*. Ed. John Bell. Oxford: Oxford University Press, 1985.

———. *The Poems of Wilfred Owen*. Ed. Jon Stallworthy. London: Hogarth Press, 1985.

Palmer, Pauline. *Contemporary Women's Fiction: Narrative Practice and Feminist Theory*. London: Harvester, 1989.

Paris, Michael. *Warrior Nation: Images of War in British Popular Culture, 1850–2000*. London: Reaktion, 2000.

Peace, David. *Nineteen Seventy Seven*. London: Serpent's Tail, 2000.

Pellew, C. Kenneth. 'Analogy in *Regeneration*', *War, Literature and the Arts*, 13, 1/2 (2001): 130–146.

Pykett, Lyn. 'The Century's Daughters: Recent Women's Fiction and History', *Critical Quarterly*, 29 (Autumn 1987): 71–77.

Ramsden, John. 'Refocusing "The People's War": British War Films of the 1950s', *Journal of Contemporary History*, 33, 1 (1998): 35–63.

Rawlinson, Mark. 'Wilfred Owen', in Tim Kendall, ed., *Oxford Handbook of British and Irish War Poetry*. Oxford: Oxford University Press, 2007: 114–133.

Remarque, Erich Maria. *All Quiet on the Western Front*. Trans. Brian Murdoch. London: Vintage, 2005.

Rivers, W. H. R. *Instinct and the Unconscious: A Contribution to the Biological Theory of the Psycho-Neuroses*. Cambridge: Cambridge University Press, 1922.

———. *Conflict and Dream*. London: Kegan Paul, Trench, Trubner & Co, 1923.

Rosenberg, Isaac. *The Poems and Plays of Isaac Rosenberg*. Ed. Vivien Noakes. Oxford: Oxford University Press, 2004.

Roth, Philip. *Exit Ghost*. London: Jonathan Cape, 2007

Rushdie, Salman. *Imaginary Homelands: Essays and* ^991. London: Granta, 1991.

Sassoon, Siegfried. *The Complete Memoirs of George* 1937.

———. *The War Poems*. Ed. Rupert Hart-Davis.

Saunders, Nicholas J. *Matters of Conflict: Material* World War. London: Routledge, 2004.

Scarry, Elaine. *The Body in Pain: The Makin* New York: Oxford University Press, 198

Schwartz, Joseph. *Cassandra's Daughter: A History of Psychoanalysis in Europe and America*. London: Allen Lane, 1999.

Schweizer, Harold. *Suffering and the Remedy of Art*. New York: SUNY Press, 1997.

Seltzer, Mark. *Serial Killers: Death and Life in America's Wound Culture*. London: Routledge, 1998.

Shaw, Philip. 'Abjection Sustained: Goya, the Chapman Brothers and the *Disasters of War*', *Art History*, 26, 4 (2003): 479–503.

Shepherd, Ben. *A War of Nerves: Soldiers and Psychiatrists 1914–1994*. London: Jonathan Cape, 2000.

———. 'Digging up the past', *Times Literary Supplement*, 4851 (22 March 1996): 12–13.

Sherry, Vincent, ed. *The Cambridge Companion to the Literature of the First World War*. Cambridge: Cambridge University Press, 2005.

Showalter, Elaine. *The Female Malady: Women, Madness, and English Culture, 1830–1980*. New York: Random House, 1985.

Sillars, Stuart. *Art and Survival in First World War Britain*. London: Macmillan, 1987.

Simpson, David. 'Iwo Jima v. Abu Ghraib,' *London Review of Books*, 29, 23 (29 November 2007): 25–27.

Sontag, Susan. *Regarding the Pain of Others*. Harmondsworth: Penguin, 2004.

Steiner, George. *In Bluebeard's Castle: Some Notes Towards the Re-Definition of Culture*. London: Faber, 1971.

Stevenson, Sheryl. 'With the Listener in Mind: Talking about the *Regeneration* Trilogy with Pat Barker', in Sharon Monteith, Margaretta Jolly, Nahem Yousaf and Ronald Paul, eds, *Critical Perspectives on Pat Barker*. Columbia, SC: University of South Carolina Press, 2005: 175–184.

Swift, Graham. *Waterland*. London: Picador, 1984.

Thomson, David. *The New Biographical Dictionary of Film*. London: Little, Brown, 2002.

Todman, Dan. *The Great War: Myth and Memory*. London: Hambledon, 2005.

Walsh, Michael J. K. *C.R.W. Nevinson*. New Haven: Yale University Press, 2002.

Westeman, Karin E. *Regeneration: A Reader's Guide*. London: Continuum, 2001.

Whelehan, Imelda. *Modern Feminist Thought*. Edinburgh: Edinburgh University Press, 1995.

head, Anne. 'The Past as Revenant: Trauma and Haunting in Pat *Another World*', *Studies in Contemporary Fiction*, 45, 2 (Winter 136.

Williams, Gwyn A. *Goya and the Impossible Revolution*. London: Allen Lane, 1976.

Willis, Paul. *Learning to Labour: Why Working Class Kids Get Working Class Jobs*. Farnborough: Saxon House, 1977.

Wilson, Elizabeth. *What Is to Be Done about Violence against Women*. Harmondsworth: Penguin, in association with the Socialist Society, 1983.

Winter, Jay. *Sites of Memory, Sites of Mourning*. Cambridge: Cambridge University Press, 1998.

Wymer, Rowland. *Derek Jarman*. Manchester: Manchester University Press, 2005.

Wood, Nancy. *Vectors of Memory: Legacies of Trauma in Postwar Europe*. Oxford: Berg, 2000.

Yeats, W. B. *Yeats's Poems*. Ed. A. Norman Jeffares. London: Macmillan, 1989.

Young, Robert J. C. *Postcolonialism: An Historical Introduction*. Oxford: Blackwell, 2001.

Zizek, Slavoj. *Violence: Six Sideways Views*. London: Profile, 2008.

Zweig, Stefan. *Beware of Pity*. Trans. Phyllis and Trevor Blewitt. London: Pushkin Press, 2000.

INDEX